*To Rufus Chambers,
Harrell Glisson and
a new generation
of Transitioners.*

Books authored by Wicke Chambers and Spring Asher

Business Books
*TV/PR: How To Promote Yourself, Your Product,
Your Service or Your Organization on Television*

Wooing and Winning Business
Como Hacer Presentaciones Exitosas (Spanish edition)

Lifestyle and Children's books
The Celebration Book of Great American Traditions

What's Up for Kids in Atlanta and Georgia; 10th Printing

The Lip Smackin,' Joke Crackin,' Cookbook for Kids

The Money Making Book for Kids

Acknowledgements

Since 1951, the Emory University Center for Lifelong Learning has provided non-credit adult education courses to the community, offering more than 350 courses quarterly on topics ranging from language and history to personal finance and business.

We'd like to thank Steve Stoffle, Executive Director, Center for Lifelong Learning, and Mary Cobb Callahan, Co-Manager of the Center's Academy for Retired Professionals and a former Director of Evenings at Emory. They gave us the opportunity to be a part of their nationally recognized program through the Reinventing Retirement class, the newsletter *Renew*, and the development of this book.

The list of *Celebrate Retirement* contributors, classmates and friends is amazing. Here are just a few:

Charlenne Carl
The Weather Channel

Marla Church
Elan Corporation

Robert Carpenter
Georgia Power Company

Mark Feinknopf
Feinknopf, Macioce, Schappa Architects

Beth Jones
Skyland Trails

Sandy Kohl
Coldwell Banker Real Estate

Derek Moore
Lockheed Martin Corp.

Jack Rosing
Atlanta Merchandise Mart

Ken Schumann
Ciba SC

Darryl Smith
AT&T

Rick Wheeler
Procter & Gamble Co.

Carmen G. Woodson
Geriatric Nurse

Lawson Yow
Smith Barney

Pegram Harrison
Attorney-at-Law

Dianne Houston
Cobb Energy

Anne Berg
Rich Foundation

Anna Berry
Southwire Company

Walt Turpening
Craftsman

Joel Alterman
IBM

Mallard Holliday
Cox Communications

Spring Asher
Speechworks

Glenn Ruffenach
The Wall Street Journal

Kelley Green
The Wall Street Journal

Pat Winchester
CBIZ-Benmark

Roy Long
Southwire Company

Don Chapman
Tug Manufacturing

Buck Stith
Stith Construction

Knox Massey
WestWayne, Inc.

Ruth White Wells
King & Spalding law firm

Nancy Dixon Bellows
Dixon Tom-A-Toe

Myrtle Davis
Atlanta Water Utility Service

Critt Graham
Critt Graham & Associates

Tarver Lowe
nVision Studios

Keith Dunnavant
Solovox Publishing

Selina Winter
Element K

Pam Holliday
Editor

CONTENTS

CHAPTER 1

Celebrate Retirement, the Freedom and the Frustrations

Life without work is a second chance to get it right. It is the time to discover the cowboy… musician … artist in you. It is the opportunity of a lifetime to discover the things that give meaning and purpose to your life, and to discover what makes *you* come alive.

Every business day approximately 15,000 American engineers, staffers, line operators, CEOs, entrepreneurs, and a host of other workers retire. They leave work with well-honed talents, experiences, training, and a heck of a skills base to use in exploring the possibilities of their new life.

Celebrate Retirement, the Freedom and the Frustrations, helps you to enjoy the freedom from day-to-day business responsibilities and to handle the unexpected psychological and emotional frustrations of being separated from the people and purpose of the corporate mother-ship.

The Genesis for *Celebrate Retirement*

This book is the result of a myriad of lively, good-humored Reinventing Retirement classes held at Emory University's Academy for Retired Professionals over the past five years. Each class has added new ideas and fresh insights on how to celebrate the freedom and deal with the unexpected frustrations.

The authors continue their mission to help transitioning professionals adjust to retirement through ever-expanding research, conference participation, and interviewing experts in the field.

The Ultimate Question

The adjustment to this new phase of life began with the question, "Now What?" It was an especially perplexing question five years ago for two wet-behind-the-ears retirees with Type-A personalities. One was an entrepreneur and the other was a corporate exec.

The challenge to celebrate their new freedom and deal with their frustrations led these two to launch the Reinventing Retirement classes at Emory University's Academy for Retired Professionals; to publish *Renew*, a newsletter *for* retirees *by* retirees that became part of the Emory Academy's web site; to find their class included in a cover story in The *Wall Street Journal's Encore* supplement for the over-55 crowd; and to view a segment on Tom Brokaw's NBC *Nightly News* show featuring one of their "first-year retiree" class members.

The story of how these events came about is best told by the Entrepreneur and the Corporate Exec.

The Entrepreneur's Story
Wicke Chambers
Retire, *hell*!

I didn't want to retire from life. I just didn't want to show up for work on a daily basis any longer.

My business partner, Spring Asher, and I had been Emmy award-winning TV producers, written six books, been business columnists in *The Atlanta Constitution* and launched Chambers & Asher Speechworks, a successful communication firm with clients nationwide. Even though the work was fascinating, I was growing tired of getting up at the crack and traveling hither and yon.

I wanted a rebirth, a renaissance of spirit. I wanted to enjoy my third stage of life and sow the seeds of my own legacy. I wanted to contribute, get involved in a new way, become an adventurer, feel celebratory and yes, even feel young and sexy. Well, maybe I won't achieve *every* one of my goals.

I was turning – no, facing a big birthday – and I couldn't decide where I belonged. Some of my clients and friends had decided to retire. I was suddenly faced with the "shoulds" and "coulds." I *should* stop and enjoy our new house in the mountains. I *could* travel more if I didn't have to show up every day, but on the other hand … ah, the dilemma.

As soon as I had spent my first six celebratory months in retirement – sleeping late, reading two newspapers, going to exercise at a far more decent hour, cleaning out closets, wandering through an unscheduled day – I began to wonder, "What have I done?"

My husband was still working, so I had no running mate. My own children, all three of whom lived close by, were at the busiest times of their lives. My grandchildren were in school or at sports. I was home alone.

At the end of the eighth month my husband and I took off for a weekend in our house in the mountains. My husband breathed the clear, sweet air and began to relax from a bruising week. I, on the other hand, hadn't been there 20 minutes when I got the prickly wiggles and thought, "What in the Sam Hill do *I* have to get away from?"

The Corporate Exec's Story

Cheryl Stephenson

Wicke pondered her retirement. I simply saw a window of opportunity and leaped through, joining the legions of corporate America's early retirees.

After 23 years as the senior public relations officer for Southwire Company, an international wire and cable manufacturer, I was at the top of my game. I loved work. It was interesting, exciting, and challenging.

I led a creative team that was among the best in the industry, honored over 90 times for communications excellence. Not only were they talented, they were crazy and creative and made work fun.

Retirement wasn't in sight. In fact, except for the monthly contribution to my 401(k) plan, it wasn't even a blip on my radar screen. Then life threw me a curve. An unexpected divorce upended my personal life while a labor strike and a corporate restructuring brought chaos to my work life. A one-two punch and the joy was gone.

When the company offered early retirement, I saw an irresistible opportunity. I confidently stepped forward, amazed at my luck and eager to celebrate whatever life had in store for me.

My retirement goal was predictable: all play and no work. It didn't take long to realize that I didn't really know *how* to play, and that my potential playmates were still doing 8 to 5 with no time off for good behavior.

My case of the prickly wiggles soon morphed into panic as I looked at the gaping hole in my life where work had been.

"Retirement? *What was I thinking?*"

Are We the Only 2?

We may have differed on why we retired, but retirement was retirement and the celebration had begun and so had the frustrations. We repeatedly asked ourselves, "Are we the only two people who feel this way?" We needed good examples from others on how they processed this retirement thing. But, we had few ideas of what or how to go about it.

We were on our own. It was the *YO-YO Years*.

Embrace the YO-YO Years

We call these years in retirement and beyond the YO-YO years because You are On Your Own to make decisions.

Every other stage of life had been brimming with counselors, coaches, teachers and guides who were bursting with knowledge on how to achieve instant success. Where were the counselors? The coaches? The retirement gurus?

In wandering forays to the Internet and book stores, we searched for books, information or ideas on retirement. The only books we found focused on how to prepare financially. There was little focus on lifestyle issues and no information on what to do with our Type-A selves and our pent-up energy. Where was there information on how to get started? How to organize your time? How to adapt to this new freedom and enjoy this life that everyone dreams about?

To our surprise, we discovered that most newsstands carry publications for every market segment except retirees. We found at least 12 publications for brides and at one count there were 14 publications on tattoos!

Once you've been catapulted from a 50- to 60-hour work week to 365 Saturdays there is a *red hot* need for guidance.

Celebrate Retirement **is about managing the retirement transition.**

This book gives you the insights and "ah-has" of actual Transitioners. It is designed to help you find new meaning, new peers, new skills and adventure in this stage of life.

Launching the Reinventing Retirement Class

Then, a mini-miracle occurred. Wicke ran into Mary Cobb Callahan, a long-time friend who had become a coordinator for Emory University's Academy for Retired Professionals. This was a new focus at Emory's Center for Lifelong Learning. After a quick catch-up, Mary asked Wicke if she would teach a class.

Wicke opened her mouth and stammered, "Yes, if I can teach it on reinventing retirement." By afternoon the Entrepreneur and the Corporate Exec had committed to teaching an eight-week session.

We knew we would be dealing with people with a lifetime of work experiences, talents and accomplishments – the smart money was on letting *them* talk. We decided to facilitate and let them teach us. Together, we would figure out this retirement thing.

The Adventure Takes Off

The pioneers who filled the first class were kindred spirits. They, too, enjoyed their freedom and were surprised by the frustrations. They brought a broad range of experiences, many practical solutions, and a lot of humor about this stage of life.

Each class has been filled with doctors, computer gurus, lawyers, brokers, males and females, singles and couples. They've come from corporate giants such as Proctor and Gamble, Lockheed Martin, Smith Barney, and The Weather Channel. And they've come from real estate agencies, schools, small businesses and big government. Their ages spanned 35 years, from 47 to 82. Some were approaching retirement; others were 5 to 15 years into the process.

Three Quick Discoveries

We quickly made three "ah-ha" discoveries:

First, no one liked the word "retiree." They felt that the term "Transitioner" described them best, and that's what they've become as they embrace their YO-YO Years.

Second, the classmates were focused on finding interesting challenges in their YO-YO Years. Contrary to what most non-retirees believe about retirement, interesting challenges – not leisure – were essential to feeling fulfilled. Deciding to become a docent, start a new business, soar in a hot-air balloon or learn Spanish are personal choices, not corporate charges. Being in control of our lives makes us feel productive and alive.

Finally, we were bowled over by the realization that retirement is not about age or gender. It's about a stage of life. Retirement is a process, not a one-time event. The transition may last six months or six years and the adjustments are the same whether you are 47 or 82, male or female!

Celebrate Retirement, the Freedom and the Frustrations is Their Story

Each class has contributed to the ideas and information in this book.

Together they determined the key chapters. First, they dealt with a profound shift in identity, the confusion of whether to work for pay or pleasure, and the issue of time management when there is more time than tasks. They discussed how to develop new interests, how to renew satisfying relationships with family and friends and how to find significant ways to give back.

Read this workbook a day or two at a time.

Use the Discovery Exercises to help you learn more about yourself, your likes and dislikes, how you feel about leaving work, how you want to fill your time and what kind of support system you need to carry you through the transition. In short, these exercises help you take a personal inventory of the person you have become. Use them like an archeologist who is looking for clues from the past to sort out the possibilities for the future. Don't let the simplicity of the exercises fool you. Put thought into your answers and you'll realize that the deeper you go, the clearer your understanding of what's important to you will become.

Study the Solutions from Survivors Q&A's. They touch on a wide range of transition issues and provide answers to some of your most frustrating questions. These survivors know from experience that most people don't make the transition from one life to the next over a weekend. It takes time to sort through years of sidelining your personal life.

Use Your Freedom to Celebrate Your Yo-Yo Years

If you are in the midst of your own journey into retirement, stick with us.

This book is designed to give you new ways to celebrate your freedom, ease your frustrations, empower you to be bold in making meaningful choices, and to energize you to use your corporate skills to discover new peers, exciting interests, and purposeful work.

Many participants have repeated the classes; some as many as four sessions. One of the newcomers was shocked to hear this and asked, "Why?" The Transitioner quickly answered, "Because retirement keeps changing, and I want to keep reinventing myself."

Loose Ends

Notes

_____

_____

_____

Questions

_____

_____

_____

Ideas

_____

_____

_____

Favorite Resources

_____

_____

_____

Things to Share on the Web Page CelebrateRetirement.com

_____

_____

_____

CHAPTER 2

Personal Identity

Only in the Witness Protection Program can you come up with a new identity quickly. And that's with the help of the FBI.

The rest of us struggle as we transition from work to whatever. Our work identity was based on what we were – doctor, CEO, teacher, chef. Our new identity isn't about what we were, but who we will become.

Retirement gives us the freedom to grow, explore and discover a fuller, more personally rewarding life, and to learn, for the first time, how we feel about a variety of things.

Now is the time to drop the work façade and tap into the real you. The forgotten you. The cowboy… artist… musician… you. And, it is there.

Michelangelo said it best, "I saw the angel in the marble and I chiseled until I set him free."

And so it is with your new life.

Celebrate Your Work Identity

If you were with a company for 20 or 30 years, don't set sail from work without a bon voyage event. Co-workers want to express their thanks to you for being their mentor, their guide, their co-conspirator or just their friend. They want to tell war stories and laugh about the good, bad and unbelievable times you shared. Invite your family as part of the celebration. It's an opportunity to celebrate your work identity and end one era before you launch the next.

What Makes Losing Your Work Identity So Tough?

- How do you handle the external and internal identity crises?
- How do you answer the "What do you do?" question?
- What is your new measure of success?
- Can your former title keep you from creating a new identity?
- How can you discover what makes you tick?

The External and Internal Identity Crises

When you walk out of the work door into retirement your

18

professional reputation is frozen in time. The world continues to define you by what you did: a graphic designer, a communication coach, an aerospace executive or whatever your last business card read.

Internally, however, there is a struggle brewing. Without the trappings of your job, the power of your paycheck, and a clear path ahead, you may suffer identity anxiety. "I went from a peacock to a feather duster overnight," laughs one Transitioner.

"After I retired I lost my self identity," said Alan Barnes, CEO of Aircond Corporation. "It took a long time to realize that *I* was having the identity problem, not the rest of the world."

We expect to go from one identity to the next, but it doesn't happen immediately. The dreaded question, "What do you do?" or "What are you doing now?" comes up in a wink at church socials, cocktail parties or civic gatherings. Answering this question is difficult, particularly for those who have been closely identified with their jobs.

This perceived loss of identity occurs only in your mind. Relax, the world is not thinking about you as much as you might think.

Get an Identity Card

Get an identity card while you figure out who and what you will become. This card serves as your retiree transition card. Include the basics: your name and how to get in touch with you. Printing the card is not hard. Figuring out what you want to say on the *next* card is. Don't worry. Cards in retirement are like golf tees. They're the cheapest part of the game and if you want to try out several labels, have fun with it.

Our Reinventing Retirement classmates are great at coming up with creative solutions to the card problem. One computer guru's new card introduced him by the slip number he holds at his vacation marina. Another turned his family into a team and announced himself as "Head Coach, The Performance Family." Another card read "SME, Computer Graphics." SME is an acronym standing for subject matter expert. This woman had retired from the day-to-day business, but she was still free to consult with others for pleasure or profit.

Travelers like cards announcing summer and winter addresses, e-mail addresses and phone numbers. Cards work well for keeping in touch with new acquaintances.

Having a card (or two) helps Transitioners begin to redefine themselves.

What Will Your New Card Say?

_____

_____

_____

_____

_____

The Search for a New Measure for Success
Charlenne Carl

Charlenne Carl had a successful career in advertising and marketing and a reputation for being a top producer when she transitioned from The Weather Channel to retirement. She vividly recalls the sense of inadequacy she felt when she was no longer working toward well-defined corporate goals.

"Taking early retirement at age 55, I was enthusiastic with the feeling of freedom to do what I wanted at my own pace. And for nearly a year, I was satisfied daily with my accomplishments – completing activities from a long-pent-up personal demand list. Then with the activities completed on my personal list, the slump hit. *Now* what do I do with my time?

"The measures of success rewarded in the corporate environment were leadership; recognition for successful execution and desired results; productivity and performance. Having spent many years in this pattern of defining personal success and worth, I was not prepared for the ambiguity I would feel in retirement when I lost that mechanism.

"What happens when the day goes by and there are no *tangible* results? This was a new and unsettling experience for me. The guilt of 'wasting time' on frivolous pursuits, the feeling of inadequacy because I wasn't meeting *my* performance expectations made me realize I had to change *my* expectations – to redefine *my* measures of 'success.' I had to recreate who I was and what made me satisfied and proud of myself.

"And, that became the new challenge of retirement, my new performance goal."

Don't Let Your Former Title Keep You in a Box
Derek Moore

You may have earned a living in one field, but your heart may be in another.

"Just because you have spent your life being known as an engineer or scientist or lawyer or accountant, don't let people keep you in that box," advises Derek Moore, retired aerospace executive, Lockheed-Martin Corporation. "Most of us are multi-talented individuals and retirement is a time to enrich our lives by exploring other things. We may be a good fit for our career stereotype, but who knows what we might become if we climb out of that box?

"Although I was always interested in art, I chose the science path at the age of 14 and have spent most of my waking hours since then in things related to science, engineering and management.

"In my transition, I've delved into watercolor painting and memoir writing. I enjoy travel with my wife and we enjoy the history associated with the places we visit. I have joined a Fine Arts group and am enjoying new people and expanded horizons.

"Some people do not even know that I'm an aerospace engineer who spent over 40 years in the business."

Begin by Discovering Your Hidden (or Neglected) Identities

The YO-YO Years are filled with changes and transitions. It takes time for a caterpillar to become a butterfly. Most business people are on speed and want a new identity overnight. So did the caterpillar.

Fast-paced, high-energy professionals take a very narrow view of themselves. They think of themselves only in a business capacity and ignore the rest of their accomplishments, talents, skills and knowledge.

We each enjoy many titles and identities. Some can translate into a new direction. Some, like husband, father, grandmother or friend, need nurturing. Others, like interests and passions, take longer to uncover.

Discovery Exercise 1

Who Are You?

Instructions: Fill in the blanks below, giving special attention to your identities outside of work. If you can't list 10 on the first pass, come back to it later. Or, ask for family members' input. Their suggestions may surprise you.

Name: _____

Last job title: _____

List 10 other identities: (Father, grandmother, golfer, artist, traveler, Rotarian, etc.)

1. _____

2. _____

3. _____

4. _____

5. _____

6. _____

7. _____

8. _____

9. _____

10. _____

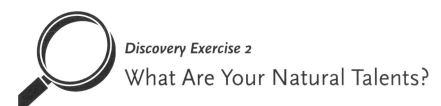

Discovery Exercise 2

What Are Your Natural Talents?

Each of us is blessed with a wide array of natural talents. Some are good at research, some sizzle in sales, others are big picture thinkers. Review the lists on the following pages and discover what traits are intrinsic to you. What makes you feel good and qualifies you to make notable contributions?

Opportunities to engage in a variety of activities may come to you as your transition puts you back in the "Available" market. DON'T be seduced by a quick opportunity to "do something."

"It would have been easy to 'default' and go back to work," said one manufacturing executive. "Work was safe and comfortable – a habit. But I wanted to see what else I was made of and could contribute. Believe me, it hasn't been easy, but I wouldn't change the process for anything."

Choose from as many categories as you like. Most people are multifaceted and versatile. This process is designed to help you discover what gives you pleasure, absorbs your interest, and makes you come alive.

You're on the road to discovering the new you!

Instructions: The following categories list personal characteristics. Review them carefully and circle all that apply to you.

STAYING ON TRACK

Fixing things   Taking a practical approach
Growing things   Building trust
Being objective   Managing things
Adding order

INTO THE DETAILS

Methodical   Operating things
Taking an orderly approach   Organizing projects
Doing the figures   Being disciplined
Making systems work

INVESTIGATIVE

Proccssing things
Discovering resources
Putting the pieces together

Analyzing information
Translating information
Asking questions

MAKING THINGS HAPPEN

Making deals
Persuading people
Making things happen
Managing things
Developing the potential of others

Making introductions
Networking
Selling ideas
Making deals

INSPIRATIONAL

Seeing the possibilities
Facilitating change
Healing wounds
Listening

Motivating others
Empowering others
Giving care
Making people feel special

CREATIVE

Being innovative
Being visionary
Making simple changes
Solving problems creatively

Designing things
Creating events
Breaking molds
Being resourceful

Discovery Exercise 3

Using Your Talents

The following exercise will help you determine how to use the talents you identified in Exercise 2.

Before doing the exercise, study the example below. Note the many ways someone can use the talent of "persuading people."

Top Choice: Persuading People

Action Steps:

1. Write grants for Welcome House, a shelter for battered women. Soliciting contributions requires persuasive communication.
2. Join the Humane Society and encourage people to spay and neuter their animals.
3. Serve on the Visitation Committee at your local place of worship and encourage others to attend.
4. Run for public office. Share your vision with others and ask them to support you financially, work on your campaign and vote for you. Use your skills of persuasion to effect positive change in your community.

Instructions: Now it's your turn. Review the characteristics identified in Exercise 2 and in the space below list the five things you do best.

Top Five Talents

1. _____

2. _____

3. _____

4. _____

5. _____

Action Steps

Instructions: Select three of the five talents and list below the persons, groups or agencies that can use this talent and why they need it.

Talent 1 _____

Names   Benefits

_____   _____

_____   _____

_____   _____

Talent 2 _____

Names   Benefits

_____   _____

_____   _____

_____   _____

Talent 3 _____

Names   Benefits

_____   _____

_____   _____

_____   _____

(On separate sheets, repeat this process for your other talents.)

Discovery Exercise 4

Polishing Your Talents

Some of your talents are razor sharp. Others may need polishing before you take them on the road.

What can you do to develop and use the talents you identified in Exercise 2? Take lessons? Get a degree? Practice? Become an apprentice?

Instructions: List the things you need to do to enhance the natural talents you identified. For example, if you excel in "persuading people," you may want to take a course on "closing the sale." If your strength is "fixing things," a technical degree in auto mechanics may be just what you need to launch a new endeavor.

Talent   Way to Improve It

_____   _____

_____   _____

_____   _____

_____   _____

_____   _____

_____   _____

_____   _____

_____   _____

_____   _____

_____   _____

_____   _____

_____   _____

Re-tire (ri tir')

[fr. retirer - *re*-back + *tirer*, to draw] 1. to go away, retreat or withdraw to a private, sheltered place. 2. to go to bed. 3. to give up ground, as in battle; retreat; withdraw. 4. to give up one's work, business career, etc., especially because of advanced age.

Solutions from Survivors on Personal Identity

Q. I hate the word "retirement." As soon as I say I'm retired, people think I'm unemployed, uninteresting and unable. Isn't there another word?

A. Is there anyone who doesn't bristle at labels like "retired," "elderly," "aging," and "senior?"

We like "Transitioner" because it describes movement and change and alludes to what you are *becoming*. But, there are many other intriguing descriptions for people in this life stage: experienced, seasoned, skilled, master, mature, active, or just everyday words like talented, versatile, capable or adventuresome.

You can be a Renaissancer, an Ageless Explorer, working for pleasure, or in new life pursuits.

Q. I climbed the corporate ladder for 35 years to the exclusion of almost everything else. Now the ladder is gone, and so is my sense of purpose.

A. Retirement can be difficult for those who've always defined themselves by their work. Becoming CEO of Your Life, Inc., spending time catching up on neglected personal affairs, searching for absorbing interests, enhancing your exercise regime or building your network of friends and family will give meaning and purpose to your retirement and challenge you in ways you never imagined.

You can bring all your corporate skills to bear on living life to the fullest.

Q. I've never been at a loss for words until now. I'm stumped and a little defensive when people ask, "What do you do?"

A. Responses to the "What do you do?" question vary with the asker.

For an intriguing, shocking or surprising response, you might try "I do whatever I want" or "I pump iron." Use your creativity by preplanning answers to the "What do you do?" question and enjoy the responses they generate. They can be real icebreakers.

Q. I've been in management for 30 years. Now that I'm retired I'm interested in being a photographer's apprentice. My wife thinks this is beneath my dignity and would be underutilizing my skills. What should I do?

A. This is your wife's issue, not yours. She needs an attitude tune-up. She's going through an identity "adjustment" created by your retirement. She says being a photographer's apprentice is beneath your dignity; however, it's her *own* status that is being threatened. Be sensitive to her feelings, but pursue your interests. It's your retirement.

Think about a trade-off. If you've changed your stripes, she needs a reason to brag or clap. Discuss a photography trip to her favorite city. Join a photography club with spouse events. Acquaint her with famous photographers. Support an interest of hers.

Q. I'm having a tough time adjusting to retirement. Any suggestions?

A. Get a retirement buddy, preferably one who has recently retired from another organization and is going through the same adjustment.

Get a retirement buddy. Guys as well as girls need a friend as they go through the stages of this transition.

Guys as well as girls need a friend as they go through the stages of this transition. First to grieve the loss, then to whine and gripe, and finally to plot the future and discuss goals. No two people can be manic depressive at the same time. Having a buddy ensures that when one is down, the other will drag you back to good times.

Q. I wore a suit for 25 years. Life was simple. Now that I'm retired, I'm having a tough time identifying my new "uniform."

A. Carmen, the model, was quoted in *AARP, the Magazine* as saying, "When I was younger, I dressed to fit in. Now I dress to stand out."

When Transitioners don't seem to fit in anywhere, they "cocoon dress." Like caterpillars they wrap themselves in clothes that are comfortable and protective – sweats, workout clothes, or worse – that are often worn several days in a row.

Now is the time to simplify your wardrobe. Keep a suit for professional meetings, weddings and funerals. Have one or two snappy casual outfits for dinner and sporting about, and buy a nice outfit for golf or exercise.

Get some red hot shoes, a cool sports watch or an Elton John pair of glasses for those days when your identity takes a fling.

Charles Schulz's Philosophy

1. Name the five wealthiest people in the world.
2. Name the last five Heisman trophy winners.
3. Name the last five winners of the Miss America contest.
4. Name ten people who have won the Nobel or Pulitzer Prize.
5. Name the last half dozen Academy Award winners for best actor and actress.
6. Name the last decade's worth of World Series winners.

How did you do?

The point is, none of us remember the headliners of yesterday. These are no second-rate achievers. They are the best in their fields. But the applause dies. Awards tarnish. Achievements are forgotten. Accolades and certificates are buried with their owners.

Here's another quiz.   See how you do on this one:

1. List a few teachers who aided your journey through school.
2. Name three friends who have helped you through a difficult time.
3. Name five people who have taught you something worthwhile.
4. Think of a few people who have made you feel appreciated and special.
5. Think of five people you enjoy spending time with.
6. Name half a dozen heroes whose stories have inspired you.

Easier?

The lesson: The people who make a difference in your life are not the ones with the most credentials, the most money, or the most awards. They are the ones that care.

– Charles Schulz

Loose Ends

Notes

_____

_____

_____

Questions

_____

_____

_____

Ideas

_____

_____

_____

Favorite Resources

_____

_____

_____

Things to Share on the Web Page CelebrateRetirement.com

_____

_____

_____

CHAPTER 3

Work for Pay or for Pleasure

Work has changed. A century ago family, community, sports, religion and hobbies occupied the mind of the American worker. The paycheck was the reason to stay in the rat race.

Today, work has become the center of life for many. Telecommunication allows people to work in favorite locales rather than offices. Cell phones make instant communications a reality around the world and around the clock. There is little opportunity to separate work from personal life.

For some, work families have replaced traditional families. People marry later, divorce or become widows. Real families often are scattered across the country. Clients, co-workers and industry associates become friends. They are the ones who go out with you after work, drop you off to get your car repaired, or prop you up when you get jilted.

For others, however, the invasion of work into their lives after 40 or so years is enough. They want out. An early retirement package or an opportunity to sell the business is the ticket out. They feel that there is more to life than the world of work. They are "a work in progress" themselves, with a sense of adventure that hasn't been tapped by work alone. Retirement speaks to them as an opportunity for exploration and growth.

Whether you fall into the "hate to leave" or "raring to go" camp, it's important that you understand the role work played in your life. An early consideration for most Transitioners is whether to become a working retiree.

What Makes the Decision to Work or Not to Work So Tough?

Do you need the money for survival? If so, hit the streets fast while your skills are still fresh. If not, and the money for retirement is available, in large or small amounts, then the questions change.

- What emotional or psychological needs did work meet?
- Do you have confidence and experience in managing your own time?
- Are you stronger working for yourself or at the direction of others?
- Are you tired of working full-time?
- Could you do what gives you satisfaction on a part-time basis?

What Emotional or Psychological Needs Did Work Meet?

The classes spent time discovering benefits they got from work other than income.

1. Their *identity and status* came from the title on their business cards. Job titles like chairman, vice president, teacher, director of, engineer or the "person in charge" gave them a status and recognition. Being a volunteer for something wasn't the same thing.
2. Work provided a *network* of contacts, associates and sometimes friends. Working meant that you were constantly surrounded by people. The silence of being at home was palatable.
3. Work offered a sense of *purpose*, a goal. But, they recognized that it is not the only avenue for achieving success or something worthwhile.
4. The engine of American economy runs on efficiency. Work provides *structure* and tells you where you'll be tomorrow and often where you'll be a year from tomorrow.

Is It Still Called Work if You Don't Get Paid?

Employment is satisfying the needs of others by offering your physical and mental activities for pay. Employment comes in a variety of sizes and shapes from full-time to time-to-time.

Work, on the other hand, is almost always a labor of love that satisfies your needs. It's any physical or mental activity exerted to make or do something, to solve a problem, to shape or forge a makeover or a new structure.

Whether it's for pay or pleasure, what matters most is what works best for you.

Retirement Jobs Are Just the Ticket for Some

An American Association of Retired Persons (AARP) study found that eight out of ten baby boomers say they intend to work at least part-time in their retirement. The reasons are as varied as the jobs.

One of the primary reasons these Transitioners plan to return to work is for the income. They realize that, after they've drawn a paycheck for 20 or 30 years, life without one can be a little unsettling, regardless of the size of their nest egg. A post-retirement job can supplement retirement and social security income or simply provide extra cash for entertainment or travel.

Another reason Transitioners clock back in is for benefits. Having a company share the cost of health insurance coverage can make a big impact on your budget and your peace of mind.

Other Transitioners miss being in sync with the rest of the working world. Why sit at home while friends or spouses are still involved with their careers? Returning to the workplace can keep you involved while adding a little jingle.

Many miss the job itself. Caring for pre-schoolers, running a corporation or purchasing the materials that make a manufacturing plant hum, gives life meaning and a sense of purpose.

Others miss the teamwork of bringing in a project on time or landing a big account. A few panic at the thought of having nothing to do and run to the nearest Human Resource office at the earliest opportunity.

A New Frontier in the Working World

Employment in retirement is different from career employment. Few Transitioners who take full-time jobs return to 50- to 60-hour workweeks and most prefer reduced responsibilities. Part-time work is the most common choice for retirees: it can be project work, seasonal work or reduced hours.

Others relish the opportunity for new challenges and dive headlong into new ventures.

A Band of Businessmen

Roy Long, Don Baker, Jim Blevins and Roger Brown

Early retirements gave these four business associates, each with 25 to 30 years of international business experience, the chance to create something new.

They formed ExP+, a management and technology consulting firm that offers big league advice for growing small businesses. They assembled a pool of retired, senior level management and technical professionals, none of whom wanted to work full-time, and today offer a broad range of business solutions to a growing client list.

"We are engaged in business again, staying abreast of emerging technology, and most importantly, using our talents to make productive contributions," said Roy Long.

What began four years ago as part-time project opportunities, is moving toward full-time involvement, enjoyment and profitability.

Walt Turpening

Walt Turpening was a geologist by education who found himself doodling with furniture designs in business meetings. "I had made some pieces for friends and worked out design problems as a hobby woodworker. Woodworking and weaving friends critiqued my work and made suggestions."

He used his transition time from the oil and gas "bidness" to create a labor of love and a business of his own. Walt is now a sought-after designer and creator of hand-woven wool and hardwood sofas, chairs, stools, bar stools and knitter's rockers.

"Being a chair maker gives me the pleasure of designing and making what people can use. I solve problems daily. I implement the solutions, and people are happy with my work. It's a very elemental level of work that brings me great satisfaction."

Anna Berry

When Anna Berry, Vice President and Treasurer of Southwire Company, retired, she changed directions and threw her hat into the political ring, running for chairman of the local board of county commissioners. Although she

If business is cyclical and the lifespan of an organization is cyclical, why shouldn't work be cyclical? After going to the top of your career, you should have an opportunity to go from being a guru in your field to being an apprentice again. After 25 or 30 years most people lose the interest and energy necessary to perform a job. Reviving that energy requires a new focus, a new challenge, a rebirth.

had never sought public office or even been involved in a political campaign, she felt the skills she developed in her 28-year career could benefit her community.

Her bid for elective office failed, but the campaigning filled her first six months of retirement with an excitement and purpose that carried her forward. She rested, regrouped and returned to the political arena. Today she's on the job, serving her constituents as Mayor of Heflin, Alabama.

Becoming CEO of Your Life

A retirement transition period allows you to take your unique skill set into new areas of interest that offer the same satisfaction and sense of accomplishment that work did.

Many Transitioners yearn to return to a more independent way of life with no ties to employment. Long delayed interests in sports, exercise, or the arts are compelling. Others dream of becoming a photographer or a writer. Still others have a growing passion for history and travel adventures like those discussed in the book, *The 1000 Places to See Before You Die*, and plan to visit places listed in the book.

Anne Shecut

Some Transitioners leave business for health reasons that require time and attention.

Graphic designer Anne Shecut was thrust into retirement when she faced a devastating illness at age 48. She combined art therapy with physical therapy in her two-year recovery. Today she expresses herself through colored pencil drawings and gelatin printmaking, creating a lasting legacy for her loved ones through her art.

Derek Moore

"After my transition from a career as an aeronautical engineer for Lockheed Martin Corporation, I was finally able to pursue my passion for books. My wife and I set up as dealers in antiquarian books and collectibles at local antique shows. We enjoyed the dealer camaraderie and even made a little money, but something was not working for us.

"We discovered that the work interfered with other enjoyable activities, particularly weekends with family and friends. We also found that moving and handling hundreds of books for each show was more physically demanding than we expected. Taking care of local and state sales taxes and local business taxes was also a pain. After six months we reluctantly wrapped up the business.

"Overcoming our sense of failure and disappointment was difficult, but eventually we found the right approach for us. We now do our selling through an upscale antique gallery. We still have enjoyable interactions with other dealers but we are free from day-to-day operations. Our time is our own again, and we can go on buying trips and do all the other things we enjoy."

Hub Scholtz

During his transition period, a friend convinced utility executive Hub Scholtz to write a book about his life. Born in Hawaii of German parents, he was an early student at Stanford University in California before he began his climb as a utility executive.

He was in his late 70s when he taught himself to use the computer to write his memoirs. He and the friend who suggested the book enjoyed frequent lunches as they edited each chapter.

When it was completed, he had two copies printed and leather bound and gave them to his son and daughter.

Rather than financial gain, the book gave him the opportunity to grow his skills, take on a new challenge and create a legacy for his family.

Look Forward, Not Backward

Before your retirement event, make a plan for the first three months, six months, or year to keep your focus in the future not the past. Use some time to celebrate, rejuvenate, catch up, repair and get started.

Whether you decide to work for pay or pleasure, launch the next phase of life with a plan. Start thinking about what you're going to do, who you're going to do it with and what you'd like to become.

The following exercises will help you to assess some of the tough work issues in your life.

What Do You Miss Most about Work?

Instructions: List the things – big and small – that you miss about work. Here's a start: copy machine, paycheck, lunch bunch, the computer technician.

_____

_____

_____

_____

_____

_____

_____

What Gives You the Most Pleasure about Not Working?

Instructions: List the big and small things you love about not working, like Monday mornings, having time for the grandchildren, turning off the alarm clock, no hassles, movies in the afternoon, or golf three days a week.

_____

_____

_____

_____

_____

_____

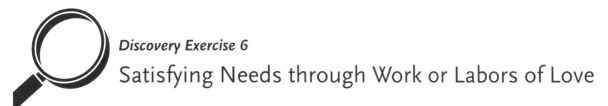

Discovery Exercise 6

Satisfying Needs through Work or Labors of Love

In deciding what work works best for you, it is important to examine your needs.

People satisfy their needs by working for profit or pleasure. They work full-time, part-time, volunteer-time or personal-time (which may even include painful time). In any instance, they want meaningful work and a sense of purpose.

The following exercises will help you identify the benefits and burdens of working — for pay or on labors of love.

Instructions: This exercise helps you sort out your needs and determine whether paid employment or a labor of love project (or a combination of the two) works best. Check either column that applies to you. Compare the two to determine which best meets your needs.

Needs	Do Labors of Love satisfy this need?	Does Employment satisfy this need ?
Income		
Benefits		
Mad Money		
Time Management		
Daily Structure		
Sense of Identity		
Status and Recognition		
Sense of Purpose		
Relieve Boredom		
Travel		
Mental Stimulation		

Needs	Do Labors of Love satisfy this need?	Does Employment satisfy this need?
New Skills		
Socialization		
Stress Relief		
Free Time		
Sense of Control		
Relieving Hassles		
Making a Contribution		
Education		
Networking		
Family		
Other Needs		

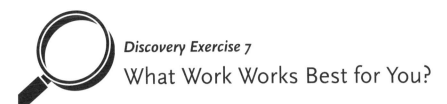

Discovery Exercise 7

What Work Works Best for You?

Paid Employment

What full-time work for salary and benefits would work for you?

_____

_____

_____

_____

What consulting, part-time work or project work would work best for you?

_____

_____

_____

_____

Labors of Love

What volunteering, caregiving, friend-in-need work would work for you?

_____

_____

_____

_____

What classes, hobbies, activities or skills would work for you?

_____

_____

_____

Solutions from Survivors
on Work

Q. I took a corporate package, but now I realize that I'm not mentally prepared for retirement. I don't have to go back to work, but unless I find something challenging to do, I may.

A. Since birth, our lives have been controlled by others. Parents, teachers, coaches, spouses, bosses, clients and a multitude of others have directed what we did and who we have become.

The day you stop work is the first time *you* take control of your life. It's tough to become the boss of your life.

Begin by asking yourself: What do I do well? Who could use this talent? What are the risks? How will I reward myself? Who do I most enjoy being around? Who would be a good mentor?

You can make a difference in many places other than the business world. The first days of work were disorienting. So is the retirement transition. Work on creating new interests and friends slowly and enjoy the adventure.

Q. I don't like calling myself a "consultant." I feel that's another word for an executive who's lost his job. What other word can I use?

A. *Roget's Thesaurus* offers several appealing alternatives: advisor, counsel, counselor, coach, expert, personal advisor or professional. "Specialist" is often used in the medical field, but others have referred to themselves as a "communications specialist" or "practitioner." Our favorite is SME, the acronym for subject matter expert.

Q. My husband wants to retire but I'm not ready. How can I defend my position?

A. If you're just hitting your stride and love your job, there are plenty of financial reasons to stay put.

Healthcare benefits are the number one reason. Then consider the financial implications – the family cash flow, your pension, your social security, your income taxes and benefits, and the tax-deferred retirement accounts that your job offers.

If, however, a potential *lonely at-home spouse* is the issue, then you'll have to get creative and help him find purposeful work that absorbs his time. Consider taking more time off, finding volunteering-with-a-purpose opportunities for him, or asking him to help with family needs. Encourage him to write a life story for his family or research his genealogy.

Q. I am about to retire. What's the best way to transition my clients to others in the organization?

A. Customers don't like surprises. One bank executive sent a letter prior to his retirement. In the letter, he thanked his clients for their business, talked about his plans for retirement and explained how the bank would care for the customer in the future.

Give yourself enough time to allow customers to consider your replacement and their options. Don't leave customers shocked when they call to do business. Bringing closure to your job not only helps customers, it helps you move forward, too.

Q. I miss the control of running a company. I'm at a loss of how to redirect my energy.

A. Retirement is tough for those who are accustomed to controlling others. But, the good news is that because you have directed a business, you may be better prepared to take control of this new situation. "Making things happen" is a strong part of who you are.

Because of the time you've invested in your business, you've had little time or energy to focus on outside interests. Take your time to search for a new direction. As you know, the Reinventing Retirement class was begun by a retired entrepreneur and a corporate exec who discovered that retirement could be frustrating and were determined to make this phase of life a celebratory opportunity.

Discovery Exercise 11 will help identify what makes you mad, sad and determined. Use it to chart a path to make things right. You are good at bringing about change. Something or someone needs your smarts.

Q. Help! Now that my husband has retired he's started meddling in my small business, literally. How do I handle this?

A. Just because he's stopped working doesn't mean he's stopped thinking. If your spouse has any financial stake in your business, his meddling may come with a sense of entitlement or expectation.

Four ideas to consider:

1. Find an area of the business that he is good at and direct him to take over this portion. Ask for a franchising strategy, a new marketing plan, hiring and firing guidance;
2. Find a new outside interest that will take him out of the office and away from staff and client involvement;
3. Be direct and address the problem head-on; or
4. Save the marriage and sell the business.

Q. I took early retirement six months ago after working since I was 16 years old. I feel guilty because I'm able-bodied and not working. How do you get over this feeling?

A. Scott Adams, creator of *Dilbert*, said in an interview with ABC News, "I think that whole workaholic thing is a myth. I don't know if we work harder than Europeans or Asians. But, I know when two people get together, they always talk to each other about how hard they work. So, Americans might not be the hardest workers. But they could be the most outrageous liars."

The world of work is like running in a marathon. The runners are focused, driven, and well trained. When the time comes to leave this competition, some focus on shorter races, others walk and still others—who feel as though they have accomplished their goals—learn to saunter.

Sauntering is hard for hard-chargers. It takes time, a changed outlook, and a new focus to dispel the guilt. Sauntering can give you a chance to discover new aspects of yourself that you've whizzed by on the way to the office.

Loose Ends

Notes

_____

_____

_____

Questions

_____

_____

_____

Ideas

_____

_____

_____

Favorite Resources

_____

_____

_____

Things to Share on the Web Page CelebrateRetirement.com

_____

_____

_____

CHAPTER 4

Time Management

For most Transitioners, having the time to do what you want when you want to is part of the celebration. Spending your time in pursuit of long-neglected interests makes you come alive.

Some are activity addicts who brag, complain or both that they are "busy, busy, busy." They say they've never been busier in their lives and don't know how they ever managed while working.

Others get prickly when there is anything on their calendars. They enjoy the flexibility and freedom of their new life. They treasure reading, playing golf, hiking, or working at their easel or woodworking bench until they feel satisfied.

Transitioners who have spent 60-plus hours a week focused on work often find having so much time to fill is frustrating. Each is suddenly faced with 365 Saturdays a year and, thanks to today's healthier lifestyles and medical advances, the realization that they may spend more time in retirement than they did in their career.

The sudden release from an office calendar or a personal data assistant (PDA) is a tremendous adjustment. People whose lives are governed by meetings, deadlines, due dates, quotas and quarters have very little time to discover what really interests *them*.

It takes courage to take control of your own life, to set your own agenda after years of having it set by others.

Why is Time Management Tough?

On days when there seem to be more time than tasks, Transitioners have those *What have I done?* doubts. They fret over questions like:

- Have I strayed from the corporate herd?
- Am I wasting time?
- Am I lonely or just happy alone?
- Could I be depressed?
- How do I wrestle those workaholic urges?

The classes discussed these questions. The following are some of their suggestions.

Straying from the Herd
Marla Church

Most of us are engineered to work, achieve goals, and amass money. We have little experience handling free time. Even on vacations cell phones, e-mail, computers – the umbilical cords of the office – keep the "connected junkies" from taking control of their own time.

Marla Church, transitioning patent attorney, had been part of a dual career marriage for 30 years. She says, "our lives consisted of sharing challenges, juggling schedules, rearing children, riding the highs of our accomplishments and licking our wounds following the disappointments.

"I was the first one to opt out of the workforce," she said. "The adjustment took time. My husband was up and out in the morning. I was home alone and suddenly I didn't feel part of the team. That first year was tough. It seemed like I was sidelined."

Being out of sync with the working world produces anxiety, a fear that if you're not "busy" you're not valuable. You've strayed from the herd. If you've strayed from the herd (norm) you must be lost, wandering aimlessly.

This fear is in your head. People are not judging you constantly. Those who ask what you're doing are anxious to have the freedom to do the things *they choose* rather than being at the will of others.

Staying busy is not the goal. Repeat: *Staying busy is not the goal.* Filling your time won't make you happy. It won't satisfy your soul. It takes purposeful activities and meaningful relationships to give joy to your days.

Chapter 5, Discovering Interests and Passions, helps you explore the interests of your choice. Be an apprentice, an explorer, a learner. Retirement is a Goldilocks time when you can try one thing and then another until you figure out what's "just right."

The Guilt that Comes from "Wasting Time"
Charlenne Carl

"My corporate life was defined by creating products – tangible outcomes – for someone else's use. I was measured on successfully meeting someone else's needs," says Charlenne Carl, transitioning Marketing Director for The Weather Channel. "When I left work, I lost that mechanism."

Many goal-driven classmates admitted they, too, felt they were wasting time when they were not pushing toward some work-related goal. Reading, painting, visiting a friend were guilty pleasures that didn't give satisfaction initially.

One Transitioner described how she had to redefine success to include all of the new things that made her come alive. "My new definition of success – my personal mission statement – is 'to use my creativity to enhance my life and the lives of others.' With a new yardstick I no longer feel guilty when I cook for company, help a friend paint his barn, read a detective story, daydream or play computer games."

The Difference Between Being Alone and Being Lonely

Many Transitioners can't discern the difference between being alone and being lonely. After years of working at the direction of others, it is difficult to turn inward and determine what's important to you.

Being alone is a special time to take stock, to stay at the driving range until you drop, or to work in the garden till nightfall. It's your time to listen to "that still small voice" and see if what you hold dear inside matches what you do on the outside.

Being lonely creates a sense of being forlorn and friendless. When you're lonely, you feel abandoned. Everyone experiences this feeling at some time. When you feel lonely grab your computer and head for the crowd at Starbucks. Go to Home Depot or Chico's and talk to the sales clerks. Become a sports fan, learn the stats and head for the ballpark.

Two single women in the Reinventing Retirement class loved to ballroom dance and lamented the fact that they had no partners. The class was diligent in finding groups for them that didn't require a partner. A single man who had joined a choral group invited others to join or come and enjoy the music. Others found hiking mates and dinner partners.

On the other hand, if you feel you are heading for depression, take control. While you were busy at work the medical world was discovering effective means of dealing with this problem.

Suspect Depression?

One of the toughest subjects we talked about in class was depression. One by one people talked openly about their experiences and admitted to feeling varying degrees of depression. Beth Jones, a class member, volunteer and board member at Skyland Trail, a mental health facility, gave us an overview on the subject.

"Every year more than 18 million Americans suffer from some type of depressive illness. Events ranging from retirement to the death of a loved one can contribute to clinical depression. It's normal to feel sad because of such events; however, sadness that continues over a long period of time may require professional help.

"Untreated major depression can seriously disrupt social relationships and activities. The hopelessness and emotional pain that can accompany severe depression can seriously compromise a person's ability to care for himself and can increase the risk of suicide.

"Depression is one of the most treatable of all medical illnesses, and treatment for depression really works. More than 80 percent of people with depression realize successful results with medication, psychosocial therapies, or both. The earlier treatment begins the more effective it can be. Generally, treatment for major depression is sought about six months after symptoms are first experienced."

Know the Symptoms

Depression affects people in different ways. Some of the symptoms that you may notice since retirement are:

- Fatigue or loss of energy;
- Irritability and restlessness;
- Reduced appetite and weight loss; or increased appetite and weight gain;
- Indifference to very important situations;
- Loss of interest or lack of pleasure in activities, including sex;
- Difficulty concentrating, remembering, or making decisions;
- Feelings of guilt and hopelessness; a sense of being worthless; and
- Chronic irritability.

If you feel that these symptoms may relate to you or a Transitioner you love, get help! There are many sources and resources available. Begin with Skyland Trail, The Georgia West Mental Health Foundation, at 404-315-8333 or *www.skylandtrail.org*.

The Blues Brothers Panel

A Skyland Trail seminar on depression featured columnist Art Buchwald, author William Styron, and "60 Minutes" correspondent Mike Wallace. All three of these panelists have suffered from depression. Buchwald dubbed them "The Blues Brothers."

Check out the workaholic's site on the Internet. www.workaholics–anonymous.org.

The Fuqua Center for Late Life Depression, another reliable resource, can be reached at 404-778-7777, or through Emory University's web site at *www.emoryhealthcare.org/fuqua*.

Resources at The National Mental Health Association are available at 703-684-7723 or by going online to *www.nmha.org*.

Who do you know who could benefit from these services?

_____

_____

_____

Workaholics Anonymous World Service Organization

Yes, there is help for the workaholics of the world. Keeping a workaholic away from the office is as hard as keeping a shopper away from the sales.

Use your transition to change environments. Cities are filled with the hum of the business engine. The "Suits" are armed with briefcases, laptops, cell phones, and all the trappings of their trade.

Bad for your rehab.

Head for the ocean, a college campus, a Habitat for Humanity site, a foreign city, or a backpack trail. You may go nuts for a while but slowly you may begin to calm the inner beast.

Take a friend or a spouse with you. It's part of the cure for a Work-Anon, a person who is in a relationship with a workaholic.

Moving from the Mental Stuff to Managing Your Stuff

Pegram Harrison

Transitioning attorney Pegram Harrison reflects on managing his personal business. "There are all degrees of work in retirement and I still 'work' dealing with litigation, radio station management, paying bills, accounting for taxes, investments, and doing endless tasks which possessions impose on us.

"It seems like a vast horde of ducks pecking constantly at my ankles."

Being time-rich, probably for the first time in your adult life, allows you to deal with the long-neglected personal stuff that pecks at you. Create a new space and place that becomes command central for organizing personal and volunteer projects, planning trips, researching new interests, exploring lifelong learning classes, playing FreeCell. It is also the place where you will have the time to redefine yourself and create your new definition of success.

Working tools should include pens and pencils, envelopes, mailing packets, staples, stamps and a file drawer. "Nice to haves" are a separate phone line, a computer and a small TV. (Chances are that no matter how attached you are to that big, ugly office desk and chair, they won't gain entry into the home zone.)

For years your personal papers have likely been crammed into drawers or stuffed into cabinets. Taxes are in one spot, files in another. Retirement gives you the time to get control of your personal business so you can move on to more enriching activities.

A Man's Cave is His Castle

Robert Carpenter

Robert Carpenter, a retired Georgia Power executive, manages his time from his cave.

"My cave is my retirement office. In my transition I personally manage more than I did before retirement, therefore an office is essential for effective time utilization and management.

"Calling it a 'cave' and the idea every man should have one, came from John Gray's book, *Men Are from Mars, Women Are from Venus*.

"It is the place for my computer, printer, copier, fax, separate phone lines, CD music system for listening to country and classical music. I have a recliner and sofa that fit me and no staff to hassle me. Almost all sports watching occurs here. Janet, my wife, claims that the TV in the den will not receive sports programming. Other cave activities include: management of investments and money, reading, scheduling tee times and making other phone calls, email and computer research, and naps.

"My cave was decorated, furnished and equipped with this in mind. In retirement if I did not have a separate room for my cave, the den would become my cave. This makes for a harmonious relationship with my wife. Our arrangement is that my office is my cave and the rest of the house is her cave. This is a compromise on her part, since before retirement the entire house was her cave.

"As a preventive measure to becoming 'activity addicts,' we decided to clear our calendar and reschedule only those things we really wanted to do. A cancelled enrichment seminar was replaced by visiting a Ritz Carlton lakeside resort for lunch. A canceled golf tournament freed us to accept an invitation to our granddaughter's fifth birthday party.

"This is the way life is intended to be!"

Manage your Time by Meeting your Needs
Lawson Yow

Lawson Yow, transitioning Smith-Barney broker, retired at age 81. "I decided I only wanted to commit to one activity a day and leave the rest of my time free for my wife, tennis, furniture making, or whatever else I wanted to do."

Lawson structured his week so that he could enjoy his freedom and still serve others, participate in civic organizations and go back to school. "On Mondays I make cassettes at the Center for the Visually Impaired. Tuesday is Kiwanis. Wednesdays, I'm a docent at Rhodes Hall, and on Thursdays, I go to classes at the Academy for Retired Professionals.

"The Reinventing Retirement class has been fun and beneficial for four years," he adds.

Discovery Exercise 8

Creating Your Dream Space

Let the celebration begin by creating your own space. This gives you breathing room and helps maintain your own sense of identity, control, creativity and solitude. Don't even think about sharing space.

Find shelf, closet, garage, or attic space. One may need a studio, the other an office outside the home. Begin the task by buying a book on how to un-clutter your life. Stamp out your pack rat passion. Get rid of old clothes, unused business files, trophies that have lost their meaning, lamps, kids clutter. Unburden your life.

This was a golden opportunity for office worker Bonnie Brooks. The clutter in her parent's house after their death was a drain on her renewal. She gathered "treasures" that others could use, called the American Kidney Foundation Pick Up Service and lightened her life.

Next, get a book or go online to find ways of creating leg room by building shelves, buying storage equipment, or calling companies that make big space out of small closets. Spring Asher, co-founder of Speechworks, did just that. With the company's help she converted a closet into an office with desk, files, shelves and even a gift wrap stand.

Men and women need their own space. Find it. Afford it. Save the relationship.

Possible locations:

_____

_____

Need to have: (Phone, computer, sewing machine, travel books, etc.)

_____

_____

Nice to have: (Private /fax line, TV, storage for artwork or photography, etc.)

_____

_____

Discovery Exercise 9

Time Management Math

Mallard Holliday said to his retiring Exec, "You've spent 25 years shoving your personal life onto the back burner. Now you will have time to live that life – just don't try to do it all the first week!"

Work does shove birthday parties, family reunions, anniversary trips and exercise workouts into the background. These exercises will help you take a quick look at what's on your back burner and determine how you'll spend your days.

Manage your time or someone else will manage it for you. Don't lose the joy!

Instructions: There's a business axiom that says "you can't manage what you can't measure." Identifying the "stuff" in your life will help you manage – and make the most of – your time. Check out the list of activities on the opposite page, then make your own list. Determine below how full your day is and how much free time you have at the end of the day. Only by knowing how you spend your time will you be able to manage it for a fulfilling retirement.

	Example	*Your Hours*
Hours to fill	24	24
Minus Sleep	– 7	–
Hours Remaining	17	
Maintenance Duties	– 5	–
Hours Remaining	12	
Family & Friends	– 3	–
Hours Remaining	9	
External Interests	– 4	–
Hours Remaining	5	
Internal Interests	– 3	–
Hours Remaining	2	
Other	– 0	–
Hours Remaining	2	

The Stuff of Life Table

Maintenance	Friends & Family	External Interests	Internal Interests	Other
Eating	Parents	Paid work	Hobbies	Travel
Bathing	Children	Consulting	Arts	Surgery
Driving	Grandchildren	Classes	Exercise	
Cooking	Siblings	Volunteering	Computer work	
Cleaning	Stepchildren	Committees	Research	
Laundry	Significant Other	Boards	Genealogy	
Grocery shopping	Caregiving	Sports groups	Scrapbooks	
Dr./Dentist visits	Friends	Hobbies & arts	Personal projects	
Rehab	Birthdays	Spiritual	Pets	
Taxes	Anniversaries		Nap	
Bill paying	Reunions		TV	
Investments			Solitaire	
Exercise			Sort photos	
			Shopping	

List Your Activities Here.

Maintenance	Friends & Family	External Interests	Internal Interests	Other

Solutions from Survivors
on Time Management

Q. My adjustment to retirement is a lot harder than I thought. I seem to be on a roller coaster of good and bad days. Will this pass?

A. Eventually. Retirement is not an event, it's an evolutionary process with several stages:

- *Pre-retirement* — Some people plan, others are too busy or in denial about the possibility. (It's like those young couples who blithely say, "Oh, this baby won't change our lives.")

- *Retirement* — This one day or one month event is often a busy celebratory stage. Getting packed up and out of the office is a whirl. Check out the movie *About Schmidt* with Jack Nicholson for a real life perspective.

- *The Honeymoon Stage* — Welcome to freedom and fun, where every day is a vacation. Sleep late, travel, play golf, do nothing. You've earned it. Too much free time isn't as easy to adapt to as you might think, however. You'll find that your to-do list simply won't fill the 2,500 hours a year that work filled. Most retirees don't look beyond this stage.

- *The Goldilocks Stage* — Goldilocks tested many things before she found what was "just right." Now is the time to explore a variety of activities and interests in search of a satisfactory fit. You may discover "This Internet class is too slow." "That gardening project is too expensive." Keep trying things until you find the right fit.

- *The "Yikes, what have I done?" Stage* – Almost everyone who can't find his or her niche or passion reasonably soon gets discouraged. This, coupled with job loss, can be devastating until you determine to succeed in retirement like you did in business. You are not alone and you can determine your future.

- *A New Pace and Place* – Moving from success to significance takes time. It takes nine months to create a baby. There are no statistics about how long it takes to create a new you.

- *Reinvention* – You may reinvent yourself many times in retirement during the course of a longer, healthier life. The exercises in this book will help you work through each new you.

Q. I've been retired for nine months and frequently find myself doing things that mimic work: scheduling appointments, working on my computer, attending civic club meetings, wearing business clothes, etc. Is this normal or am I having a harder time adjusting than most?

A. It's very normal. Old habits are hard to break and the routine of performing them gives comfort.

Try easing into a new schedule. At the top of your calendar list all the fun things you want to do. Join a photography class. Schedule a mentoring opportunity. Help a friend launch a new business. Take charge of a high school fundraising effort or visit a war memorial. Add these to your calendar whenever there are empty slots. There are week-long immersion classes in arts, language and travel. Sign up for one to *crowd* your calendar and help you break those old work habits.

The Mayonnaise Jar Ah-Ha

A professor stood before his philosophy class and had some items in front of him. When the class began, wordlessly, he picked up a very large and empty mayonnaise jar and proceeded to fill it with golf balls. He then asked the students if the jar was full. They agreed that it was.

So the professor then picked up a box of pebbles and poured them into the jar. He shook the jar lightly. The pebbles rolled into the open areas between the golf balls.

He then asked the students again if the jar was full. They agreed it was. The professor next picked up a box of sand and poured it into the jar. Of course, the sand filled up the remaining space. He asked once more if the jar was full. The students responded with a unanimous "yes."

Now, said the professor, "I want you to recognize that this jar represents your life. The golf balls are the important things – your family, your children, your health, your friends, your favorite passions – things that if everything else was lost, and only they remained, your life would still be full. The pebbles are the other things that matter like your job, your house, your car. The sand is everything else – the small stuff.

"If you put the sand into the jar first," he continued, "there is no room for the pebbles or the golf balls. The same goes for life. If you spend all your time and energy on the small stuff, you will never have room for the things that are important to you.

"Pay attention to the things that are critical to your happiness. Play with your children. Take your partner out to dinner. Go out with friends. There will always be time to clean the house and fix the washing. Take care of the golf balls first, the things that really matter. Set your priorities. The rest is just sand."

One of the students walked up to the front, produced two cans of beer and poured the entire contents into the jar, effectively filling the space between the sand particles. The professor asked what he was doing.

"Professor," he replied "I just wanted to show that no matter how full your life may seem, there's always room for a couple of beers."

– Author Unknown

Loose Ends

Notes

_____

_____

_____

Questions

_____

_____

_____

Ideas

_____

_____

_____

Favorite Resources

_____

_____

_____

Things to Share on the Web Page CelebrateRetirement.com

_____

_____

_____

CHAPTER 5

Discovering Interests and Passions

Now that you've retired you'll have plenty of time to follow your interests and passions. But, anyone who has ever faced 50- to 60-hour workweeks, family demands, mortgages and a myriad of other pressures has had little time left for outside interests.

If given the opportunity, most people would go out and buy an interest just to eliminate the hassle of finding one.

> *Being busy is easy.*
> *Being satisfied is what*
> *gives joy to your days.*
> Satisfaction comes
> with purposeful
> work and meaningful
> relationships.

When Transitioners emerge from the black and white world of business or the professions, they discover they have acquired many amazing, Technicolor talents along the journey.

Now is the time to develop the *all* of you. Answering the *Now What??* question gives you a chance to identify those activities that absorb your time, stimulate your mind, and develop your potential.

Early on, it's important to sample all kinds of activities. Like Goldilocks, you'll soon know if the activity is too big, too boring, or just right. But be careful. Prolonged flitting from one activity to another keeps you distracted, dissipates your energy and leaves you feeling restless. *Meaningful* interests are the cornerstones of new directions.

What Must Be Considered in Discovering New Interests and Passions?

According to class discussions, there are a number of issues to be considered when discovering your interests and passions.

- What interests and subjects intrigue you?

- How can you best develop those interests?

- How can you expand those interests into group activities?

- What things absorb your time daily?

- Are you willing to take risks?

Explore the Possibilities
Benjamin Franklin

At the age of 42 this successful printer retired from business. It was actually the midpoint of his life. He didn't feel that he needed to keep working just to build a bigger nest egg.

Franklin had an insatiable curiosity and he cherished the thrill of discovery. He had a keen interest in scientific fields even though he didn't have an academic background. He was considered by some to be a "dabbler." That never seemed to bother him. His "tinkering" in electricity led to the discovery of static electricity, the lightning rod, the first electric battery, and many other practical inventions including the Franklin stove. He used his good sense (expressed in *Poor Richard's Almanac*) and diplomatic qualities to launch many other civic and national achievements.

Franklin demonstrated an eagerness to know about a lot of subjects. Use your curiosity as a powerful stimulus for discovering and pursuing new and meaningful challenges and interests.

Expand Interests You've Kept on the Back Burner
Dr. Peter Mark Roget

Mark Roget was a philologist, scientist and physician. When he retired from medicine he decided to use his newfound leisure time to continue developing a list of synonyms he had begun earlier to help him be more precise in his speaking.

Mark Roget's retirement project became a thesaurus. Since 1852, *Roget's Thesaurus* has never been out of print.

Discovering Your Passion
Mary Kay Ash

After a successful career in direct sales, Mary Kay Ash retired and decided to write a book to help women survive in the male-dominated business world. She soon realized that the plan she was devising was a great business plan for herself!

In 1963 she took her life savings of $5,000 and with her son's help started Mary Kay Cosmetics. She wanted to create a nontraditional employment opportunity for women to set their own hours, work around family and other commitments, supplement their income, or be a primary income source. Today Mary Kay Cosmetics is a Fortune 500 company with annual sales exceeding $1 billion. Over half of the national sales directors earn over $1 million a year.

And Now, Back to Your Life. What Absorbs You?

In his book *Finding Flow, The Psychology of Engagement with Everyday Life*, psychologist Mihaly Csikszentmihalyi talks about discovering how to feel fulfilled in our everyday lives.

Human beings feel best when they are challenged. New or abandoned interests provide a variety of challenges. Golf games, book discussions, mentoring, working a crossword puzzle or learning to use power tools tax our skills and absorb our attention.

Consider those times when you lost all track of time because you were so totally absorbed in untangling a problem. Concentration creates flow. The tougher the problem, the deeper the involvement.

"When I bought my first computer I remember the salesman saying, 'Keep a clock nearby. You'll be amazed at how the hours zip by before you look up.' I was totally absorbed, challenged and fascinated by what I could learn. I was in the Flow daily," said a transitioning teacher.

Life daily presents a fresh supply of interests and challenges, from dealing with the water bill to coping with new health issues. Each demands concentration and problem solving skills. Use your newfound time to improve your finances, health and life.

Master the Detours

If you are dogged by distractions or have a problem with procrastination, divide and conquer the problem. Take mini steps to a major accomplishment.

Aristotle said, "Whatever we learn to do, we learn by actually doing it. Men become builders by building and harp players by playing the harp." If you want to learn a new computer program, divide the manual and read a few pages a day. Do you want to master digital photography? Take five digital photos and work on the picture-perfect printing of each of them.

Concentration replaces doubts and fears. Working for the joy of it, rather than for the bottom line, is empowering.

Changing directions from the world of work and finding new interests takes time. Don't rush it.

Continue the Search for New Interests

Sandy Kole

Sandy Kole, transitioning from Coldwell Banker, teaches computer classes to older users. But, she needs more of a challenge for herself. "I bought a digital camera and am taking a class in Photoshop. I'm in a class with photographers and I'm learning a lot from them, but what I really wanted was the challenge of learning a new way to use my computer."

Hang up the cell phone, turn off the TV, and log out of Solitaire. Challenge yourself to run a half-marathon. Develop three gourmet menus to prepare for friends and family. Sign up for an outdoor adventure trip. Search out-of-town newspapers for innovative ideas to use in your community. Ask your grandchild to teach you to play his favorite Xbox game. Learn to play chess online.

Meaningful pursuits demand concentration and build skills. The struggle revs up mental muscles and releases endorphins.

Return to Those Thrilling Days of Yesteryear

If things in your current life don't seem to rev your engine, hark back to those thrilling days of yesteryear.

If you allow yourself to become jaded because you've seen it all, then head back to some of the interests that gave you pleasure as a child. Those passions can smolder and simmer for a long time before you decide to throw your arms around one and commit to a plan of action.

Revisit some of your pet pleasures and discover new ways to lose yourself in your revitalization.

Retirement gives you 2,500 hours each year to get into the flow.

Sam Posey

Sam Posey, Grand Prix race car driver, retired from competition shortly after his son was born. The birth of his son rekindled his childhood passion for scale model trains.

He documented this growing passion in his book, *Playing with Trains, A Passion Beyond Scale*. What is amazing about this book is how Posey's curiosity in a subject spawned so many paths of discovery.

He first explored new scale models and train designs, layouts, and suppliers of scenery, equipment and tools. He then expanded into the history of model trains, tools, travels, magazines, and catalogues. Each stage awakened his imagination and revved up his enthusiasm.

It took 15 years to create his masterpiece: an exact replica of the Colorado Midland Express Railway.

Joel Alterman

Joel Alterman put away his boyhood passion for cars and baseball when he made his family and career the center of his life.

With few hobbies or outside interests, he found himself at loose ends after retiring from his job as Manager of Marketing Communications for IBM. Then he learned that Ford was reincarnating its Thunderbird.

He searched the Internet for information on this exciting new car, placed an order for one, and began talking to other enthusiasts. Today, the chat group he helped create boasts 2,000 members and the rallies and other fun-filled events he's organized have attracted hundreds of new Thunderbird owners.

But, it was his love of baseball that led to his greatest retirement achievement: the 50th Anniversary Celebration of the 1954 Atlanta Crackers. He thought the anniversary of the winning season of his favorite boyhood team should be honored. So, using his corporate skills, he planned the event, got the Atlanta Braves to provide financial support, located the living members of that great minor league team, brought them to Atlanta and held a two-day celebration that included recognition at a pre-game ceremony at Turner Field.

Through that event, he is now involved in organizing an Atlanta Sports Hall of Fame to honor Atlanta sports heroes and remember the great moments in the city's sports history.

"I've learned that the harder I look for something to do, the less I find. If I just live life and keep my eyes and ears open, ideas will come to me . . . if I'm willing to grab the bull by the horns and make things happen."

Risk Something New Every Day

Whether it's a childhood passion or a new one, never let age deter you. It's only a number. And probably if you were asked, "How old would you be if you didn't know how old you are?" you'd respond with an age 15 to 20 years younger than you are.

You've established a reputation by retirement and no one can take that away from you. The older you get the more important it is to risk something every day. New interests provide the opportunities to take risks. Stay curious. It keeps you young.

It's Never Too Late

Several years ago a group of retired Navy men whose average age was 73 had a passion to resurrect a dilapidated WWII vessel known as the *LST 325 Memorial Ship*. This ship had seen plenty of war action and had been part of the D-Day beach assault at Normandy.

The Navy was concerned about a group of "senior citizens" transporting a rebuilt ship across the Atlantic Ocean but the "old salts" were undeterred. They were determined to "sail that sucker back."

And so they did.

Life Doesn't Stop When You Stop Working
Mark Feinknopf

Mark Feinknopf, a Harvard-educated architect, spent his working years designing structures. He's spending his years after work designing non-violent communities.

A friend gave Mark and his partner, Cynthia Moe, a book by author Marshall Rosenberg. Rosenberg's message on non-violent, compassionate communication was so potent that they wanted others to have the opportunity to hear it. Instead of taking a pleasure trip to Greece, they invested $14,000 to bring Rosenberg to Atlanta to conduct a workshop on non-violent communication.

The first workshop was held at the Carter Center and Mark and Cynthia did most of the work organizing and publicizing it. The turnout was so encouraging that they continued pursuing the subject.

"By now our passion had ignited and no amount of effort seemed too great," declared Mark.

The second workshop was held at Emory University's Center for Lifelong Learning and attendance doubled. People attended from as far away as Great Britain.

Mark and Cynthia's non-profit organization, Sacred Space, now has a steering committee of 25 and plans are underway for an international workshop.

"Life doesn't stop when you stop working," says the man who has come alive through his newly-discovered passion.

It takes exploration and determination to uncover an interest. The next two exercises will help you discover many new trails to blaze.

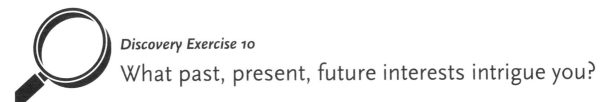

Discovery Exercise 10

What past, present, future interests intrigue you?

Present Interests

Name three things you would like to do.

1. _____

2. _____

3. _____

Name three things that you've dropped because of work, family responsibilities, and lack of time.

1. _____

2. _____

3. _____

Past Interests

Name three things you were fascinated with when you were a child.

1. _____

2. _____

3. _____

Name three things you wanted to be when you grew up.

1. _____

2. _____

3. _____

Future Interests

Name three things you'd like to explore.

1. _____

2. _____

3. _____

Name three pipe dreams.

1. _____

2. _____

3. _____

Roadblocks

List the things that are blocking your path.

1. _____

2. _____

3. _____

How can you clear the way?

1. _____

2. _____

3. _____

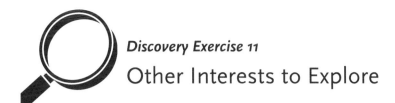

Discovery Exercise 11

Other Interests to Explore

Look for seeds of creative discontent.
What doesn't seem right in your world?

_____

_____

_____

_____

_____

Discover what makes you mad.
What neighborhood or community problem needs a solution?

_____

_____

_____

_____

_____

Where do you most enjoy spending your time?
If it's golf, maybe you're good enough to teach kids, or be a Ranger, or start a club team.

_____

_____

_____

_____

_____

Take a new look at an old business, college or creative interest that offered you pleasure but not a viable income.

A retired banker had a passion for history in college, but he also had a wife and child and needed an income so he pursued a career in another field. He used his transition years to reignite his passion. What interests did you abandon?

_____

_____

_____

_____

_____

Become an apprentice. Take one-day or one-week classes in things you're curious about.

What subjects spark your curiosity? Where can you get more information or experience?

_____

_____

_____

_____

_____

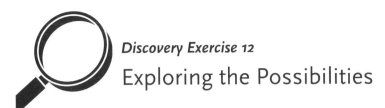

Discovery Exercise 12

Exploring the Possibilities

Now that you have identified things that interest and intrigue you, it's time to explore how these interests can be developed. The traditional way of doing this is to outline and make notes in a logical, orderly process.

That's why we're tossing out the outline and exploring the possibilities using a brainstorming exercise. Now is the time to let your imagination soar.

Take a look at the example below, done as a class project by Joann Floyd to broaden her interest in the piano.

It's amazing to see how far an interest can be taken.

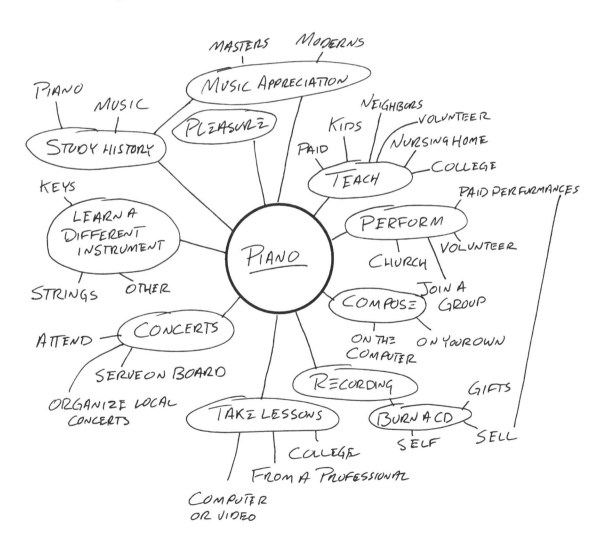

Instructions: Choose one of your interests. Write it in the center of the circle. Explore the different ways you can enjoy it. This exercise can be richer if you do it with friends. You'll be amazed at the opportunities you'll uncover when you put your heads together.

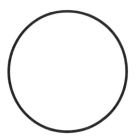

Discovery Exercise 13

Expand Your Interests

Now that you have explored an interest, expand the ideas by listing things you can do alone or in groups. Joining groups not only allows you to explore your interests but also leads to new peers and interesting relationships.

Instructions: Use the examples below to jump-start your thinking about working on your own or in a group. List your activities in the spaces provided.

ACTIVITY	SOLO	GROUP
MUSEUM	Take a tour	Become a docent
TRAVEL	Subscribe to an international travel magazine	Travel with a group tour
BOATS	Look up the history of U-Boats	Join a Power Squadron boating class
COOKING	Try a Cajun recipe from the Internet	Join a three-day Italian cooking class
FINANCE	Write a book on "Finance for Kids"	Teach a finance class to kids in Junior Achievement

Solutions from Survivors
on Personal Identity

Q. My passion has always been my work. Now that I'm retired, nothing excites me.

A. Being career-focused people causes us to push aside many things of interest in life.

Begin by making a list of 10 things you're curious about, ignorant of or want to know more about. Let your imagination run wild.

Go on the web and review these topics. Your search will lead you down many links of interest. Read magazines from other cities to discover additional topics to pursue.

Check the paper for community classes of interest. Then sign up. Even if you don't like the class you will meet new people and gain a grain of knowledge on the subject.

Fill out the exercises in this section. Sometimes an interest hits you right between the eyes. Other times an interest looks appealing but you talk yourself out of it because it's not big and beautiful or it seems an odd choice for a person like you.

Finding new interests is like finding the right job. It takes research and determination and no whining.

Q. What do you do when you've cleaned the closets for the third time, finished the honey-do list and still can't find anything meaningful to do?

A. Spend some time daydreaming.

The most remarkable thing about daydreaming may be its usefulness in shaping our future life.

Industrialist Henry J. Kaiser believed that much of his success was due to the positive use of daydreaming. He maintained, "you can imagine your future." Florence Nightingale dreamed of becoming a nurse. The young Thomas Edison pictured himself as an inventor. For these notable achievers, it appears that their daydreams gave them a vision to work toward.

If you're still stalled, work on Discovery Exercise 11 in this chapter.

Q. My passion has always been golf. Now I realize it's not enough.

A. What do golf pros do when they retire? Ask them.

Golf is a constant challenge. There is a fresh sense of challenge on every hole, every shot, each day.

Golf is also many faceted. Play a round at St. Andrews in Scotland. Visit the Golf Hall of Fame in St. Augustine, Florida. Teach at your local recreation department. Make your own clubs. Open a pro shop. Organize tournaments for non-profits in your area, or study the history of the sport.

Or do an about face. On a rainy, cold, achy day take a "cheap challenge." Head for the library and challenge yourself to find three books that pique your interest on subjects that you don't know anything about: China, new math, DNA, how to play the saxophone, oil drilling, theatrical plays, or forensic science. Challenge yourself to learn three facts about each.

Q. I've always been very responsible and honored all commitments. Since I retired I'm having trouble committing.

A. It may be that you've outgrown your interests in certain projects. When life changes directions, it's time to re-evaluate your commitments.

Do these commitments provide involvement that gives you energy? Are you in a learning situation or have you ridden the board position too long? Can someone else bring more zest to the job? And more importantly, is there something else to which you'd rather be committed? Don't hang on out of habit or fear that you'll never be asked to serve again.

You have earned the right and privilege to Just Say No, and to step aside to give newcomers a chance to get involved. Spend your time finding things that are important to you *now* and commit to them.

Loose Ends

Notes

_____

_____

_____

Questions

_____

_____

_____

Ideas

_____

_____

_____

Favorite Resources

_____

_____

_____

Things to Share on the Web Page CelebrateRetirement.com

_____

_____

_____

CHAPTER 6

Satisfying Relationships: Couples, Singles, Family and Friends

Jumpstart your transition by reconnecting with your personal friends and family members. They are the strength of your new life and the quality of these relationships will have direct impact on your health and happiness. They're the ones you reach out to when you're mad, sad, or glad. TVs and computers may be ready companions and provide hours of interesting enjoyment, but they are no substitute for a strong hand to hold or a warm body to hug.

Each Reinventing Retirement class thought that developing meaningful relationships with those who are most important to you–your spouse, significant other, children, grandchildren, parents, friends, and yourself (especially if you are single)–is the goal.

Relationships with your spouse or partner may get rocky as you go through the retirement transition. Children have become busy while you were involved with your career and may not have the same needs you remember. And, you just may find yourself becoming your *parents'* parent, an uncomfortable adjustment for all. Now may also be the time to settle family differences, deal with family skeletons or mend fences.

Mike Wallace of CBS's *Sixty Minutes* once said that he would never retire because he'd have to worry about who to have lunch with. So, if you didn't start taking inventory of your friends before you walked out of the office, now is the time to reconnect and enjoy.

Celebrate your family and friends as you leave your work family. It may not be instant or easy. Be the first to make the move.

What are Some of the Relationship Issues You Face?

Reinventing Retirement classmates spent many hours discussing the dynamics of their relationships with family and friends. The issues they identified include:

- How are you going to continue to grow as a couple?
- How can you be single and not alone?
- Should you relocate?
- How do you create a strong network of friends?
- How do you handle family expectations?

"Honey, I'm Home!"

Most couples have never spent more than two weeks together since they threw the bouquet. They've both gone about creating busy business, civic or parenting lives between the breakfast and dinner greetings. In retirement they each have expectations and fears that are real, but often *unspoken*.

Men and women have vastly different views of retirement. A man fears being bored, losing his identity, or not finding his niche. A woman fears a friendly takeover situation, interruptions to her lifestyle or a loss of independence. Both put on a game face and the children end up worrying, "My parents have been married for 30 years. One of them retired last year and I'm afraid they are going to kill each other or get a divorce."

In retirement, there will be a *lot* more time together, no matter whether one or both are transitioning. Now is the time to take a fresh look at your seasoned relationship in a 24/7 world.

Conduct a Needs Analysis

When it comes to the retirement of either marriage partner, it's time to look at the marriage in a new light. In business, when the status quo changes you conduct a SWOT analysis, considering the *strengths, weaknesses, opportunities and threats*. In marriage, we prefer to do an NSP analysis to ensure that both parties achieve a fulfilling life.

An NSP analysis addresses the *needs* each has, the *seeds* for new growth that retirement allows, and the *peeves* – the little things that make each other prickly.

This analysis can be beneficial in a variety of marriage situations:

- A working spouse and a non-working spouse.
- A retired spouse who wants the other spouse at home.
- A newly launched career spouse versus the one who's been-there-done-that and wants out.
- A healthy caregiving spouse and an ailing spouse.

Understanding and accommodating the needs of two fully-grown, experienced, talented, unique individuals brings a new sparkle to a long-time, loving relationship.

Establish a Few Ground Rules Early On
Ken and Patty Schumann

Within two months of her husband's retirement, Patty Schumann, wife of Ken Schumann, retired Director, North American Agriculture Business, Ciba Special Chemicals, AG., decided new policies and procedures were needed for family harmony. She set the following rules for him:

1. You cannot fall asleep and snore in front of the TV from 9 to 5, Monday through Friday;
2. You cannot follow me around and ask what I'm doing;
3. You cannot expect me to prepare your lunch every day; and
4. You must answer the telephone.

Patty's Rules clarified her expectations and increased harmony in the Schumann household. Ken respects that.

The men in our Reinventing Retirement classes weighed in with a less formal but just as important list for creating harmony.

1. Don't interrupt with questions while I'm working on a project;
2. Don't ask me what I'm thinking;
3. Don't tell me when to do something. Give me a list and I'll get it done at my convenience; and
4. Don't ask me what I'm thinking.

Nine Innocent-Sounding Questions

The classes agreed that the following questions are loaded for both partners in retirement. When you hear one of them, tread lightly, smile and give a good-humored response.

- What's for lunch?
- Who was that on the phone?
- When will you be back?
- Do you want me to drive you to the store?
- Why do you have the spices *here*?
- I'm sorry I didn't hear you. What did you say?
- I know you're washing the dishes, but would you hold this ladder for me?
- You want me to do *what*?
- *When* are you going to get off the phone?

The following exercises and Solutions from Survivors will also help transitioning couples. The questions answered here have been well documented, deliberated, cussed, discussed and dissected by the Reinventing Retirement classes. Unless you deal with these issues honestly, openly and quickly, poor relationships will be a constant thorn in your side and make the hours in retirement tick-tock…tick-tock.

His needs or her needs may not be your needs.

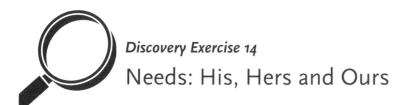

Discovery Exercise 14

Needs: His, Hers and Ours

Create a purposeful life together by understanding and addressing your individual needs and your needs as a couple.

Be sure to think about the big and small areas of your life: time, space, relocation, the TV remote control, activities and interests, community life, grandchildren, travel, household chores, spiritual life, money, friends, expectations.

Instructions: Fill out your list of needs separately, have a glass of wine, and compare notes. You both may be surprised by the results. Make defining your needs as a couple a collaborative effort.

His	Hers	Ours

Discovery Exercise 15

Seeds for New Growth

What would you most like to do, achieve, see, experience, finish, start, or accomplish? Retirement offers you the opportunity to go for it. If not now, when?

Instructions: List His and Her desired plans separately, then get together to discuss and complete the Ours section.

His	Hers	Ours

Discovery Exercise 16

Peeves

No explanation needed! In the interest of lasting relationships, please limit your list.

His	Hers	Ours

Online Personality Test

Want to have some fun and learn more about your compatibility? Humanmetrics.com offers a Jung Typology Test. Take the online personality test:

www.humanmetrics.com/cgi-win/JTypes2.asp. There may be a small fee.

Discovery Exercise 17

Know It All

Without much thought household and life responsibilities get divided between partners. One pays the bills. The other runs errands, cooks or makes travel plans. No matter how these important tasks are divided both need a solid overview. In the event that one partner is out of town, ill or dies, both need to become a "Know it All."

Instructions: Fill out the following, adding your own "need to know" items at the end.

All Computer Passwords

_____

_____

Social Security Numbers

_____

_____

Financial Information (Contact names, location and phone numbers)
    Bank Accounts

_____

_____

_____

    IRAs

_____

_____

_____

Investment Accounts

_____

_____

_____

Certificates of Deposit

_____

_____

_____

Keys to safety deposit box

_____

Debts

_____

_____

_____

Assets

_____

_____

_____

Tax Records

_____

Accountant

_____

Personal Records (Location of these documents)
   Will

_____

   Durable Power of Attorney

_____

   Living Will

_____

Other Records (Location of these documents)
   Birth Certificates

_____

   Marriage License

_____

   Passports

_____

Deeds

_____

_____

_____

_____

Other important things both spouses should know. Schedule a time and teach each other how to:
- Program the remote control
- Set the thermostat
- Prepare lunch
- Operate home theater or other electronic equipment.
- Operate the vacuum cleaner.
- Buy groceries.

Who do you use to:

Cut your hair? _____

Dry clean your clothes? _____

Repair your auto? _____

Clean your home? _____

Groom your pet? _____

What are your children's addresses, phone numbers, e-mail addresses? (List)

_____

_____

_____

_____

_____

_____

_____

_____

Other "need to know" things:

_____

_____

_____

_____

_____

_____

_____

When the focus of the
partnership shifts
from financial to
lifestyle, retirement
can be a reality check.

Solutions from Survivors
on Couples' Retirement

Q. In our 30 years of marriage, my wife and I have never spent more than four consecutive weeks together. How do we start adjusting to full-time togetherness?

A. Couples change from the bride-and-groom age to the grandparent stage while they work. Work experiences, life challenges, family, travel, and individual opportunities redefine each partner. But, this usually happens so slowly that neither notices subtle changes *until retirement*.

When the focus of the partnership shifts from financial to lifestyle, retirement can be a reality check. *He* wants to travel. *She* wants to volunteer. He needs a tennis partner and she's into horseback riding.

Try changing roles. If she pays the bills, he cooks. The exercise of swapping jobs or going from teacher to student will add new skills and a lot of humor.

Q. My husband is retiring after 25 years in management. I don't intend to be his secretary. How do I bypass this opportunity?

A. In Jeffery Sonnenfeld's book, *The Hero's Farewell, What Happens When CEOs Retire*, the author talks about a survey he took of 200 spouses of retired executives. One of them stated, "He has no one but me to order around now. I'm not his secretary, not even his temp."

There are three things you can do to ensure his successful transition.

1. Determine if his company has an office or secretarial services available in retirement.
2. Find a welcoming space at home or elsewhere

for his workspace. Ask his current assistant to help him identify his work and computer needs. Ask about company electronic set-up services. Schedule a Transition Day celebration. Get stamps and other office supplies and enjoy a special lunch. Determine who answers the phone and teach him how to take messages for you.

3. Help him make a list of people to call for lunch. Stock up on lunch favorites. Teach your executive how to cook or defrost simple lunches, then get going with activities that are important to you.

4. Be a good listener.

Q. My husband is about to retire. He's a Type-A personality. Any suggestions about division of household duties before he tries to take over our home?

A. Divide and conquer. Household chores should not divide along gender lines. Men take great pride in their efficiency in all jobs, not just repairs and remodeling.

The Reinventing Retirement class polled a group of friends and discovered that men believe that they are far better at spot cleaning and organizing laundry, have better ironing skills, and are more efficient in bagging recycled trash. Wives were rated more experienced at loading a dishwasher. Husbands were better at stacking and putting them away. Men don't cook, they become chefs and love to display their culinary skills.

Still unsure? Take your own poll of male household bragging rights. You'll be amazed at the household accomplishments claimed by many talented males.

Q. I've retired and my wife still works at a job that she loves. My buddies rag me about playing golf while she works. I do feel a little guilty. Any suggestions?

A. What's more important is how you and your wife feel about this arrangement. If she loves her work and you love golf, enjoy. Your friends are probably jealous that you get to play golf *without* trade-offs.

Q. My wife and I both want our own identity. It's hard in retirement.

A. Work gives you an identity and sense of self worth. Once you've enjoyed the sweet taste of your own success it's hard to let go of that sense of accomplishment.

Pursue your own interests and friends and become your partner's best booster in his or her field of interest. Discuss your activities at the end of the day. This will keep both of you vibrant and interesting to each other.

But don't pass up the joy of accomplishing something new together. One couple took up cycling. "It's great exercise and gives us a sense of accomplishment," they said. Another couple took up golf and helped each other improve their games.

Q. Lunch has become a big issue since I retired six months ago. My wife won't fix it and all my lunch associates are still working. Should I go on a diet?

A. Don't be afraid to pick up the phone and call a friend, a group of retired friends, a child, a neighbor, an empty-nester, or a widower. If they aren't free that day, schedule a later date. Keep a list of their names and numbers handy and keep adding to your list.

Think about someone starting a business who would be pleased to have your expertise. Look for groups like Kiwanis, a golf association, or an industry association that have regular luncheon meetings.

Make a lunch date with your spouse. Make it interesting, romantic, or in a new restaurant. A little wooing *works*.

Q. Since we've retired our lives have become mundane. How can we become more interesting to each other and have a more stimulating lifestyle?

A. Ruts are tired grooves in the road of life. If you two feel like you're in a rut, try a new road and see where your curiosity leads you.

Create a plan together. *She* becomes the tour leader and recommends a new restaurant, a museum exhibition or a different weekend trip and he reads up on the places. *He* suggests taking in a sports game and she does some research on the players and stats. Each may hate it, but the experience gets you out of the rut.

Discuss a mutual interest like gardening, music, or tennis. Read and discuss new ideas together. Invite new friends to dinner and cook the meal together – one does the meat, another salad, desert, etc. It's delightful mayhem and you will all survive. Challenge each other to come up with a new solo adventure. Discuss your adventures over dinner.

Single but Not Alone

Being single in retirement, whether through death, divorce or distance, brings a unique set of challenges to this time of life.

Instead of learning how to live with your spouse 24/7, you're learning how quiet it is when you live by yourself 24/7. Without the discipline of work, you can easily fall into the habit of staying up late at night and sleeping in the next morning. From there it's just a baby step to "Since I'm not going out today, why bother getting dressed?"

Single retirees must get up, get out, and get going! You need human contact.

What will you do with yourself? After all, work has been the center of your life and a lot of your acquaintances have been work-related. Many of them are still on the treadmill and don't have any more time than you used to have, so they are not readily available. And, although it's hard to accept, work was the bond that held you together; the farther you get from your retirement day, the less you have in common.

Single-Minded Pursuits that Suit

Finding compatible acquaintances and lasting friendships are crucial for single retirees. Consider the following suggestions for building your support network.

Reconnect with old friends. Many will be in the same place you are and will welcome a call or visit.

Look to your place of worship for opportunities to deepen former relationships and grow new ones. Join the chorus, keep the nursery, or become part of the audiovisual team.

Volunteer to help out with a community program. Whether you are serving as a docent at the botanical garden

"You get in life what you have the courage to ask for."
Oprah Winfrey

or building sets for the local theater group, you become part of the ebb and flow of life once again.

Head for the gym or join a tap dance class to celebrate the Rockette in you. You'll feel great, look great, and meet some buff new friends.

Go back to school. Learn art history, how to paint a floor cloth, or how to lay tile. The discussion doesn't stop when the class ends and there are coffee shops where you can explore the topic and get to know your classmates. You may even choose to go back to college for a degree. Some colleges and universities allow you to attend free on a space-available basis if you're over 62. The courses can be for audit or for a degree, depending on whether you want to do the exams. There's nothing like strapping on a book bag to make you feel smart and sassy again.

Now's a great time to get to know your family. You've probably short-changed them during your work career, so retirement is a good time to mend fences or rebuild bridges. Your nephew, uncle or cousin may need a helping hand on a repair project and you now have the time to be of assistance. Research the family tree (weak limbs and all) with your kin; genealogy is a great way to laugh and learn about your ancestors while enjoying each other's company.

Be neighborly. Whether you are older or younger than the families around you, get to know them better. Offer to watch their house when they're on vacation, share your garden harvest with them, or lend them a cup of sugar whether they want it or not. Be nice to their kids, even when they trample your begonias. Your neighbors are the people nearest to you and your closest lifeline in an emergency.

You have to kick-start yourself to go into a world not defined by work. Remember, you learned a lot of skills in those 30 or 40 years of work. Apply what you learned to being a single retiree.

Discovery Exercise 18

Single Transitioners' Needs

Instructions: Complete the following. Be sure to include contact information – phone numbers and e-mail addresses – for every name listed.

Relationships

Who can you interact with regularly? Phone buddies, shopping friends, other retirees, fellow gardeners, family favorites, lunch dates?

_____

_____

_____

_____

_____

_____

Team/group activities

What activities can you participate in with others to keep you from becoming isolated? Consider such things as golf leagues, book clubs, hiking clubs, travel tours, community and church or temple activities.

_____

_____

_____

_____

_____

_____

Support network

Who will you call when you need help: when you come down with the flu, have car trouble, need a ride, or hear a bump in the night?

_____

_____

_____

_____

_____

Expanded skills set

What do you need to learn to make your life as a single retiree easier and more enjoyable?

_____

_____

_____

_____

_____

Other

List anything else you feel you need to make the most of your transition.

_____

_____

_____

_____

_____

Discovery Exercise 19

Prepare a "Plan B"

When you don't show up for work, someone calls to check on you. If you don't answer the phone, they soon show up on your doorstep.

In business, having a back-up plan was *good business*. As a single Transitioner, it's important for you, too, to have a back-up plan for when the unexpected happens.

Transitioning geriatric nurse, Carman G. Woodson, suggests Transitioners living alone do these things to prepare for life's curves.

Put this emergency contact list by your bed.

Police

_____

Fire

_____

Friends

_____

_____

_____

_____

Neighbors

_____

_____

_____

_____

Doctors

_____

_____

_____

_____

_____

Pharmacy

_____

Vet

_____

Religious Affiliations

_____

_____

Home Repairmen

_____

_____

_____

Organizations (Rotary, golf association, etc.)

_____

_____

_____

_____

Make a current list of your medications

Keep it up to date. Place one copy in your wallet and one by your bedside. Give a copy to a relative or friend in case there is a hospital stay involved.

_____

_____

_____

_____

_____

_____

_____

Stock your pantry

Keep a supply of easy-to-open cans of juice, soup, and cereals that only need water. Store canned chicken and meats, instant rice, baking potatoes and frozen meals. When the ice storm hits or the virus comes knocking, you'll be prepared.

Identify a normal week's chores

List weekly household tasks like laundry, watering, taking out the garbage, dealing with kitty litter, getting the mail or washing dishes. When you're under the weather and someone asks, "How can I help?" you've got the answer.

_____

_____

_____

_____

_____

Barter

Many decades ago, bartering was common. Rural people swapped produce for a legal will or other goods and services. Bartering is alive and well today and can be quite beneficial to single transitioners. Learn to make specific exchanges; be sure you know the real costs in dollars and cents to ensure equity. (One single Transitioner bartered an attic floor installation for six homemade meals.)

Things I can provide: Value:

_____   _____

_____   _____

_____   _____

_____   _____

_____   _____

_____   _____

_____   _____

_____   _____

_____   _____

_____   _____

Set up a Durable Power of Attorney (DPA) for Healthcare

In the event you are hospitalized, ask a family member or friend to take responsibility for your medical treatment and keep a list of medications you're given.

In case of a stroke or some other incapacitating illness, give them the power to follow *your* wishes about when to come home, nursing homes, and most importantly, duration of life support. DPA forms are available online, at libraries, and at bookstores.

Solutions from Survivors
on Singles' Retirement

Q. I retired three years ago at age 60 and my spouse just died. I'm now without a job and without a partner. I can't decide whether to go back to work or not. Suggestions?

A. Studies have shown that retirees who have a strong network of friends and family adjust and thrive.

The loss of your wife has left a void in your life that will never be filled. Even so, it's important for you to connect with others in meaningful relationships. Working – for pay or pleasure – might be just the thing for you. Your mind will be busy and you will meet new people.

If you choose not to work, you'll need to find activities that involve other people. Check out Discovery Exercise 20 for a new support group. Lending a helping hand in the community will also make you feel alive again.

Q. As a business woman, I frequently – and confidently – traveled alone. Now that I'm retired, I feel more vulnerable traveling by myself. Why?

A. As a business traveler, you had a psychological safety line that kept you connected to your company. Someone always knew where you were, who you were meeting with, and what your travel plans were. They could also provide any emergency resources necessary to ensure your safe return home.

You can replicate this sense of security by soliciting the help of a family member, friend or even an associate who is an experienced traveler. Leave your itinerary and phone numbers with them, and check in daily, just as you would have with your secretary or supervisor when you worked.

Most people would be happy to be your home base, and having to *touch base* regularly will make you a confident traveler once again.

Q. I'm a retiree without a spouse or playmate. How can I alleviate the loneliness that retirement brings for singles?

A. The silence is deafening – and often a shock – for single retirees accustomed to over-the-cubicle conversations, ringing phones and humming equipment. Interaction with co-workers gives a sense of community that evaporates when your daily companions are Regis & Kelly or Judge Judy.

While a trip to the local home improvement or grocery store will give you human contact, having someone to provide emotional support, listen to your concerns and let you know that you're still valued is more important.

So, identify the people who energize you and visit with them this month. You'll be surprised what other activities are generated as a result of those contacts.

Q. I'm an introvert. Since I left work I find myself staying at home and becoming more and more isolated. I know I should get out, but I don't feel comfortable initiating anything.

A. You have to have a reason to get up and get out. Since you won't do it for yourself, do it for others. Volunteer to drive cancer patients to treatment. You'll quickly realize how blessed you are, how much you are needed, and your life will be richer for it.

Q. As a female engineer, I worked primarily with men. I would like to have lunch with one or two of them occasionally. I'm maxed out on girl talk. Should I?

A. When you've been "just one of the guys" for most of your career it's understandable that you would miss the camaraderie and the friendship of your co-workers. Have lunch with a couple of them at the *same* time. The conversation will be more energetic and everyone will feel more comfortable.

Relocation

To many, retirement means celebrating the freedom by packing up and moving on. The dream locale that has played in your head on lumpy days at work now beckons. It may be a Bed and Breakfast life, an RV adventure, a country spot with hiking at hand or a new life across the pond. If so, use the following reality check to evaluate your move.

If you intend to celebrate your new freedom as most do by digging in and enjoying your current location with family, friends and interests close by, skip this section.

Selling the house or condo can be viewed as an instant nest egg, especially if the property has increased in value. Resist the temptation to sell out and take off immediately after retirement. Instead, consider renting your current place for six months or a year and renting a similar place in your dream location for the same period. Test out the adventure and make sure it doesn't morph into a nightmare.

There are many stories about people taking off for a remote log cabin in the wilderness and going nuts, or moving to a bustling city with concerts and learning opportunities and going nuts. Reinventing yourself in your YO-YO years can happen many times, so leave space for several moves before you find "just the right spot." This is important for couples as well as for singles.

Finances, communication and family responsibilities are the keys to successfully relocating. Before you pull up stakes, do your homework and use the following questions as a guide.

Financial considerations	Yes	No	Discuss
Can you afford to retire now or would you be better prepared in a few more years?	____	____	_____
Have you considered hiring an objective, third party financial planner?	____	____	_____
Have you factored in your new dream costs?			
Cost of a commute	____	____	_____
Material and supply costs	____	____	_____
Training or equipment costs	____	____	_____

Have you checked:	Amounts
Housing costs	_____
Utility rates	_____
Insurance expenses	_____
Taxes	_____
Membership fees	_____
Relocation costs	_____

Communication Issues	Yes	No	Discuss
Do you want a change of seasons?	___	___	_____
Are the volunteer offerings interesting?	___	___	_____
Does the community have lifelong learning?	___	___	_____
Are there sports opportunities?	___	___	_____
Are community or club teams open and interested in new members?	___	___	_____
Can you find a challenging or forgiving golf foursome?	___	___	_____
Are there health care and medical facilities to keep you fit?	___	___	_____
Is public transportation available or will you need two cars?	___	___	_____
Does the community reach out to newcomers?	___	___	_____
If you are interested in travel, are you close to airports?	___	___	_____
Would the place be fun and offer growth opportunities for both?	___	___	_____

Family responsibilities	Yes	No	Discuss
Will your parents or other family members require care?	___	___	_____
Are there assisted living or nursing facilities in the area?	___	___	_____
Will you miss the connectivity of your grandchildren, siblings or friends?	___	___	_____
Can you readily find a new support network?	___	___	_____
Are there pools, sports or arts programs for your grandchildren to enjoy?	___	___	_____
Is the area pet friendly?	___	___	_____
Is there a good vet or pet sitters if you go on vacation?	___	___	_____

Celebrating Friends

The long-running sitcom *Friends* perfectly illustrates the need for friends in our lives. Friends may fight with you, disagree with you, spend your money and drive you nuts, but in the end they provide meaningful relationships and someone to have lunch with.

It's important to choose friends who energize and support you, introduce you to new ideas and support your causes. *One* friend and *on*e spouse will *not* meet all of your needs. Look to your network of friends to pick up some of the slack.

Friends are particularly important as you transition. Leaving the work family behind can be a set-up for isolation. Join new groups. New friends will add zest to your life. A mix of old and new friends is best.

Reunions and Reconnections

It takes time and effort to build and maintain friendships. Your newfound freedom gives you the opportunity to do some needed repair work with those you may have neglected or build a new network of interesting people.

Jumpstart your reconnection overhaul with the nearest phone or e-mail system. Lead or support a class reunion, a sorority or fraternity gathering, a family reunion, a professional gathering, a civic or business alum group. Or call four or five friends or neighbors for lunch and laughs.

Class members and others offer the following suggestions.

Reconnect with Friends

Lin Black, retired director of a special education teacher training center, reconnected with college sorority pledge sisters. After she retired she called national headquarters and

"I went to grammar and high school at Druid Hills in Atlanta, and have enjoyed reunions immensely. There weren't many cameras in the fifties and the reunions are my best contact with those 'happy days.'"
Terrell Jones,
Delta Airlines pilot

got a list of her pledge class with some – but not all – phone numbers and e-mail addresses. She sent out her request for a reunion, responses started coming in and then a search began for those were not heard from. The event was a success. Organizing it reconnected her sorority sisters, stirred up happy memories, and gave her a ready e-mail list.

Terrell Jones and Beth Jones, not related but good high school buddies, aided and abetted the same effort with their high school class. It's a great way to reconnect.

A group of lawyers who went through law school about the same time and who no longer attended the big gatherings at the Bar Association meetings broke into a smaller, professional group. They get together monthly at a different kind of bar. Litigators, general counselors, judges, corporate specialists are invited to membership. They gather to talk a little shop, enjoy pleasurable and painful professional memories or start up new connections. There are no projects or minutes, just good times.

Civic association luncheons or monthly business alumni meetings serve the same reconnection opportunity. Join in for the laughs and the projects that these groups may sponsor. Go. Enjoy. Find a smaller group and create your own lunch bunch and e-mail tree.

If none of these ideas suit you, check the newspapers for Brown Bag Lunch and Learns. Various groups make these offerings. Check to see if theaters in your area sponsor these events. If not, make the suggestion.

It's easy to make excuses for not attending, supporting or instigating these gatherings. You have a contribution to make and an opportunity to make someone's day. Southwire Company retiree and recent widow John Maddox said, "I've discovered that I'm not the only one who finds it hard to call old friends or new ones. But you have to do it. You have to just suck up your guts, pick up the phone and do it."

Discovery Exercise 20

Who's in Your Network?

A University of Michigan study suggests that a powerful predictor of how satisfied a Transitioner will feel in retirement is the number of relationships he or she has. Retirees who were most satisfied reported a network of 16 people, on average.

The following exercise will help you to identify the strengths and weaknesses of your network.

Instructions: List the people with whom you can enjoy 16 different activities. If there are more activities than people, get to work expanding your social network.

Who will you:

Play sports with _____

Have lunch with _____

Travel with _____

Watch the game with _____

Talk about your interests with _____

Participate in your faith with _____

Have dinner with _____

Visit with in the neighborhood _____

Catch a movie with _____

Discuss books with _____

Talk on the phone with _____

Do projects with _____

Hang with _____

Discuss investments and finance with _____

Share your problems with _____

Volunteer with _____

Teach or mentor _____

Learn something new with _____

Shop with _____

"Fix" things with _____

Fish or hunt with _____

Exercise with _____

Chew, spit, gossip, and cuss with _____

Who is your Retirement Buddy?

This is the person who's in about the same place in the retirement transition as you. It's the person who's going to experience with you the ups, downs, ins and outs of transitioning.

_____

_____

_____

_____

_____

Solutions from Survivors
on Friends in Retirement

Q. I have met many nice people since I retired three years ago, but compared to the people I worked with, they're just acquaintances. I thrive on teamwork and the bonds it generates. How can I recapture this?

A. Look for volunteer, community or academic organizations that need teamwork. The Red Cross, Habitat for Humanity, community boards, and other organizations need teams that work toward a common goal.

Offer to coordinate the team. This often requires phone calls or e-mails to set up the group. Keeping the team updated, in touch and motivated with the project is the core of building a strong team. This center position will help you build a list of new contacts. If you are good at teambuilding, this is a natural position for you.

Q. Now that I'm not as consumed with my career I'd like to get in touch with some of my favorite friends, but I'm afraid that my neglect has cut the cord. What can I do?

A. Friends from your past hold a special place. You share a common history: good days and awful days, first dates and heartbreaks. There is a comfort level that rarely requires effort.

Pick up the phone. Make the first move! Be interested in them. No whining and not too much reminiscing. Find out about their current interests, travels, family. Plan a group reunion.

Q. I want to meet people but I need help making conversation. I'm not comfortable talking to people outside the office.

A. You don't need to talk to be thought of as a genius. Just be good at asking questions. The *who, what, when, where* and *why* questions work. CNN host Larry King says that "why" is the key to his success as an interviewer.

"Whose movies do you like best?" "What sport do you follow?" "When do you think is the best time to go fishing?" "Where do you like to travel?" The *why* question works as a great follow-up question to any of the answers you get.

Don't be afraid to share experiences and stories about yourself. That's the way real friendships begin.

These questions might lead you to discover a common bond, which will get you off and running in an exchange of interests and information. Don't be afraid to share experiences and stories about yourself. That's the way real friendships begin.

Q. Relationships are built on common bonds. I'm in a hurry to speed up the process now that I seem to have a lot of time. Any suggestions?

A. Head for the gym on a regular basis. Friends who groan together, moan together and tone together build bonds fast. "Sweat" creates bonds and pulls the workout crowd together.

The gym or a local YMCA are also good places to develop multi-generational friends. Show up regularly and if you skip a session you'll be missed. Have juice together later.

Family Matters

Adult children, stepchildren, grandchildren and aging parents are the most important people in our lives because they are part of us. Sharing ourselves with them brings immense joy, and it makes us emotionally healthier and happier.

However, because we love them and feel a sense of responsibility to them, they are often the source of our greatest frustration.

Caught in the Middle

You've looked forward to the freedom and adventure of retirement, but what you may find is that you've transitioned into a life where you're sandwiched between the needs of your adult children and your aging parents.

More adult children are living at home. The reasons are varied: low starting salaries, delays in getting married, the high cost of housing, or divorce. When they move back in, some bring children, placing three generations under a roof that was pretty comfortable with just you and your spouse.

Other adult children, deep into their careers, look forward to your retirement as much as you do, seeing you as a source of extra help with their overbooked lives. Those adorable grandchildren that you never had enough time to enjoy while you worked are on your doorstep, in your workshop and at your kitchen table morning, noon and night.

Aging parents, who are coping with life changes themselves, are a concern for many Transitioners. Caring for them can be harder than you think, primarily because they don't *want* help. Virginia Morris, author of *How to Care for Aging Parents*, reminds us, "Your job is not to control your parents' lives, but to allow them to maintain as much control as possible."

Whether it's children, stepchildren, grandchildren or parents, the need for caregiving is great. Taking care of those you love takes patience and energy.

Dealing with Your Family's Expectations

Diane Houston

Diane Houston, Supervisor of Customer Care for Cobb Energy, was surprised when, as part of a retirement class assignment, she discovered that her daughters expected her to move in with one of them when she retired.

"I have my own life to live!" she said.

Diane is a dedicated member of the Red Hat Society, a group of women dedicated to fun and frivolity. She plans to celebrate her retirement by opening a tea room to combine her love of antiques with her love of people.

Derek Moore

When Derek Moore retired from his successful career in aerospace, his adult son had great difficulty understanding him.

"At a time when my son was working hard to establish his career and provide for his young family, he found it difficult to accept what he perceived as my unproductive lifestyle," says Derek.

"'What a waste,' my son was frequently moved to exclaim.

"What was I doing? I was pursuing my interest in antiquarian books, which included buying and selling. I attended lectures on art and literature and history and anything else I fancied. I was taking up watercolor painting and doing some memoir writing. I was playing tennis. I was spending time with my granddaughter. I was traveling with my wife. So, what was the problem?

"I had no problem. I was doing what I wanted to do. My son had the problem: I was not meeting his expectations. In his eyes, I was not living up to my potential. He was understandably evaluating things in terms of work and earning potential, which is how he needs to evaluate himself. The same was not true for me.

"Now that I am retired I can explore those things that give me the greatest satisfaction. I am free to define my own success and to meet or exceed my own expectations. I can change directions and not have to justify it to anyone, except perhaps my wife.

"Retirement can bring wonderful freedoms, but you have to grab them for yourself. Don't let others define your successes, no matter how well meaning they may be."

Today Derek believes his son is proud of him again. "I think he sees that 'Dad doing what Dad pleases' is something *he* can look forward to down the road."

Balancing your needs and wants with those of your loved ones is one of retirement's toughest challenges. Love them. Care for them. Do less and encourage them to do more. But don't give them your YO-YO years.

The Right Start

A good way to start is to share your dreams with your family. Let them see your excitement, enthusiasm and even your anxiety over this life change. Then ask them what they think about it. Give them an opportunity to express their feelings about an Executive Dad who no longer works or a Mom who's traded a briefcase for a backpack. Be sure to include your grandchildren in the discussion. Their voices should be heard, too.

Reconnect with your Extended Family

Family reunions jumpstart a reconnection with family members with whom you may have lost touch. Ask siblings, young cousins, and great aunts and uncles for their address lists and track down members who are AWOL. Assume the duty of making the arrangements. Get help from others with materials. Ask every family member to bring a covered dish, or get a caterer. One classmate sent invitations to a reunion touting the day's entertainment: "Talking about those who aren't here." The family enjoyed the humor and she got perfect attendance!

Spring Asher, co-founder of *Speechworks*, had a holiday gathering for her immediate family of 14. She created "Ja'maican' Me Crazy" T-shirts for their trip to Jamaica and used the same logo to make luggage tags on her computer. The T-shirts made a great picture and the trip made lasting family memories.

It's important to give your children and grandchildren a sense of family. Your life will be fuller as you get reacquainted or newly acquainted with your relatives.

Enjoy a real family network. Find out who's the family computer wiz and set up a family web site. Start with reunion photos, then expand to photos and biographical information on your ancestors. The gathering and posting will give your family a reason to stay connected.

Above all, count your blessings. Families make life worth living.

Discovery Exercise 21

What Are Your Family's Expectations?

Family issues arise when you and the ones you love have different expectations. Find out what your children, stepchildren, grandchildren and parents expect from you in retirement. Write down what they want and then write down what you want. Share your thoughts and interests with them. Retirement can be a time to reconnect and deepen your relationships, while preserving and exploring your dreams.

Instructions: Ask your family what they expect from you in retirement and write their expectations below. Use this opportunity to clarify mutual expectations.

Here are a couple of examples to get you started: My children want me to stay in my home, but I want to move to a warmer climate; my siblings want me to take care of Mother because I'm closest, but I think we should share the responsibility.

My children want me to:

_____

_____

My parents want me to:

_____

_____

My grandchildren want me to:

_____

_____

My siblings want me to:

_____

_____

Discovery Exercise 22

Family Opportunities and Issues

Whether you're helping your adult children, caring for grandchildren, or taking care of your healthy-but-aging parents, you can head problems off at the pass with a little planning.

Identify the issues you anticipate, so that you can address them. Thinking about these things now is a good way to take care of your family and yourself.

Example Opportunity: Create a "win-win" situation

Example Issue: Selling the Beach House

Example Action Step: Offer to let the children buy it outright or make the payments on it going forward.

Adult Children and Stepchildren

Opportunity to Connect:

_____

_____

Issue:

_____

_____

_____

Action Step:

_____

_____

_____

Grandchildren

Opportunity to Connect:

_____

_____

Issue:

_____

_____

_____

Action Step:

_____

_____

_____

Parents

Opportunity to Connect:

_____

_____

Issue:

_____

_____

_____

Action Step:

_____

_____

_____

Get On the Home Team

As your parents' health declines, caring for them will affect the whole family. It is important to get everyone involved: your parents, your siblings, your children and yourself.

Find out what's important to your parents, discuss the independence issue, and make sure their finances and medical and legal houses are in order. Then identify resources and have a plan.

How you go about caregiving is the difference between peace of mind and an emotional roller coaster. Share the load, ask for help and most importantly, take care of yourself.

Resources

"Caregiver University: Learning To Help Someone You Love" has been developed by WebMD Health and is available 24 hours a day, seven days a week. It provides information and resources you need to make informed decisions about all aspects of caregiving.

Caregiver University is available at *www.VistaCare.com/caregiver*.

Solutions from Survivors
on Family Matters in Retirement

Q. I retired to spend more time with my family. To my surprise, I find that they all have active lives of their own. Now what?

A. Give your family a gift by creating your own interests and cutting the dependency cord. Use the Interests and Passions Chapter to jump-start your adventure in learning. Join a group and be a contributor. Paint. Hammer. Play an instrument. Cook. Write. Get a job. And, whistle a happy tune.

Q. Since I retired I'm overwhelmed by requests to baby-sit my grandchildren or run errands for my parents. Work used to be a great excuse. Now what?

A. Every classmate experienced these new "opportunities." When asked to baby-sit or run errands or take care of the dog, the response was always the same: "Oh, Honey, I'm sorry. I have a meeting."

The class determined a better response was, "I'm sorry, I have a commitment." It might be zilch, but it keeps you politely in control.

Q. Not only am I trying to adjust to my own retirement, I am dealing with parents who are daily moving toward dependency. This isn't what I expected.

A. Unfortunately, this is one of those surprises life throws your way. Both adjustments are emotionally and physically draining. Exercise regularly to maintain your physical health, and find a friend who's dealing with the same issues to help you hang on to your sanity. While sharing your thoughts with someone who's going through the same thing may not help the situation, it will release some of the tension.

Discovery Exercise 23
A Gift of Gratitude

Instructions: List the kinds of things you do for your friends and family to show them how much you appreciate them. Visits, calls, outings, chores, hugs.

Spouse

_____

_____

_____

_____

_____

Family

_____

_____

_____

_____

_____

Friends

_____

_____

_____

_____

_____

Loose Ends

Notes

_____

_____

_____

Questions

_____

_____

_____

Ideas

_____

_____

_____

Favorite Resources

_____

_____

_____

Things to Share on the Web Page CelebrateRetirement.com

_____

_____

_____

CHAPTER 7

Making a Difference

After a successful career, it's easy to clean off your desk. But it's practically impossible to pack away a mind full of problem-solving skills and experiences. Nor should you. Consider them the ultimate retirement gift and use them to make a difference.

Making a difference doesn't have to be big and beautiful. Small deeds can make a tremendous difference in someone else's life.

When Ethel Percy Andrus retired from teaching, she became concerned with the meager state pensions retired teachers received. Her concern led to her instrumental role in founding the National Retired Teachers Association, which successfully obtained low-cost insurance for its members. From her concern for retired teachers came an advocacy for *all* retired and older Americans. In 1958, she founded AARP, The American Association of Retired Persons, which today has more than 30 million members and 4,000 chapters throughout the United States.

Although it's wonderful to impact millions of lives, making a difference doesn't have to be big and beautiful. Small deeds can make a tremendous difference in someone else's life.

As a sense of independence grows many Transitioners may not want to commit to a regular volunteer assignment. They may prefer to do their 'giving back' independently, with people or groups they know.

Almost anyone, from your parents to your neighbors to your state, can use the skills you developed over a long and productive career.

What Issues Should You Consider Before Volunteering Your Time?

These issues were singled out by Reinventing Retirement classmates as the most important ones to consider:

- What non-profit agency is the best fit for your talents?
- Should you bypass the agency route and do your "own thing?"
- How can this book help you make a difference in another Transitioner's life?

A Gift for Others, Growth for You

Jack Rosing

Jack Rosing, a Manufacturer's Representative for the Atlanta Merchandise Mart, is a people person who shares his good humor and zest for life in many different ways.

He started volunteering, as many people do, with the Parent-Teacher's Association in his children's school. Business prompted him to get involved in other volunteer capacities.

"In retirement I find that volunteering in the community, politics, medicine, and religion have broadened my horizons. You never know where joy or the opportunity to make a difference in someone else's life will happen. Don't stay at home and think joy will find you."

Volunteering at non-profit agencies works best for many Transitioners.

Finding the Right Agency Fit

When you were looking for employment, you searched for jobs that fit your talents. The same should be true with finding the right non-profit agency.

A Reinventing Retirement classmate recounts his freshman effort at giving back to his community after a very successful career. Shortly after he retired, he volunteered his services at a well-known non-profit agency, thinking he could make a difference to the children they served. His assignment was to hand out sheets of paper. "They were *blank*," he told the class.

Don't just volunteer.

Do your research. Non-profit agencies come in all shapes, sizes and types of service. Selecting the right one *for you* is just as important as the work you will do for them.

There are many sources for volunteer information. Do a web search for Volunteer Opportunities and add your city. Local newspapers often publish lists of volunteer opportunities. The telephone directory has a list of local agencies and associations that might need help. Friends and even your former employer are other sources for agency information. Finding the right fit for your talents takes effort.

There are as many agencies and organizations to choose from as there are businesses and industries to work for. Narrow the list by deciding what you're interested in. Whether you choose to work for the needy, the elderly, the animals, or the arts; for sports programs, school programs, local or national organizations, you will be able to share your skills, learn new ones, make new friends and increase your sense of gratitude.

Bill Atkins

Bill Atkins, transitioning Deloitte Consulting partner, volunteers for SCORE, Counselors to America's Small Business. A friend suggested that his consulting skills would be an asset to people anxious to start a business of their own.

"The work is very diverse," Atkins says. "Clients come in with all kinds of ideas, from starting an aromatherapy business to opening a bail bond firm. It's exciting to help these fledgling entrepreneurs develop the skills to run a business, market a product or close a sale. I am really volunteering my time to make heroes of others." Atkins adds that SCORE is especially interested in having active and retired women and minorities to serve as counselors and trainers.

Once you get involved in a non-profit agency, you will be surprised at the expanding list of needs you will uncover. You will find that the more you give back, the more you gain.

Change Direction If You or Your Talents Don't Fit

On August 14, 2000, *Fortune* magazine published an article entitled *Candy Striper–My Ass!* It was a word to the wise about the "culture clash looming as a high-powered wave of retiring executives meets the genteel world of volunteerism."

There can be issues of ego, turf, talent, bottom line goals, deadlines, and real or perceived needs that both sides must consider in order to have productive, satisfying relationships with effective results.

Agencies should ask themselves what volunteer help they need. Do they need staff support, coaching, specific skills? Or do they need volunteers who can make key business contacts, or lead a fundraising effort? Developing challenging volunteer jobs that hold the interest of the volunteer takes effort. For those agencies willing to do so, the rewards can be significant. And on the other side, understanding the organization's needs and having the right skills that add value takes time and effort on the part of the volunteer.

Before signing up, volunteers should be prepared to work at a different level and pace than in business. Building consensus is more significant (and sometimes more challenging) than building profits.

Many agencies have well organized volunteer programs. These are excellent choices for Transitioners who value the agency's work and want to contribute several hours a week to support it. Being a docent, building a Habitat for Humanity house or mentoring a student all fall into this type of volunteer opportunity.

If, however, you are a good idea person with high energy, you may want to look for an agency that doesn't have a large professional staff. Your contribution will be more valued and will interfere less with a staffer who may be trying to build his or her own reputation.

All agencies need your financial support.

Recycle Your Talents on Your Own

Recycling your talents on a one-on-one basis with family, neighbors, high school or college friends or organizations close to your heart is a great way to start. You have a whole bag of workplace skills and talents that can be used in new ways to make a difference in their lives.

Listening skills developed in sales can be a gift to parents or children. Nobody said the listening would be easy, but making someone feel heard is important.

Teaching financial skills to help Junior Achievement students understand the economics of life will refresh and sharpen your financial knowledge. Youthful questions make you dig deep.

Encouraging others jump-starts courage within. When a struggling golfer encouraged her young friend to try out for the baseball team, she found the very same words gave her the courage to try out for her club's golf team.

Taking care of cranky, aging parents will make you a smarter, kinder and more knowledgeable elder. It also teaches patience.

Lugging groceries up the steps for your neighbor is a gift for them but a muscle builder for you.

Tutoring or coaching someone who wants to learn is fun. Teaching a disinterested student, however, is a challenge that taps your best skills.

If you are good at writing resumes you could use this skill in many ways: with college students, with people who have just been laid off, or with empty-nesters who

You will find that the more you give back, the more you gain.

want to re-enter the job market. You'll be as excited as they are when they land that perfect job.

If you've been dieting and have created tasty diet snacks, teach a class on delicious dieting at a community college or write a column for a neighborhood newspaper. Food editors and readers are always looking for recipes.

If you're good with computers, art or gardening, the same kind of exercise will help you find ways to give that satisfy both you and the recipient.

Create Your Own Project

If you're a mover and shaker and don't want to be slowed down by agency bureaucracy, take a tip from Ethel Percy Andrus and do your own thing.

Consider working with other transitioning professionals. This often eliminates the agency turf issues and the fear of high-level outsiders that can threaten non-profit professionals. There is also a real sense of camaraderie and control.

Some members in the Reinventing Retirement class pooled their know-how to produce *Renew*, a newsletter on topics surrounding the retirement transition. Using corporate skills from law to layout, they forged a bond while they worked on a project to help other Transitioners.

Start a Celebration Group

If none of these giving back ideas fit your needs, and you, too, are curious about how others are managing the freedom and the frustrations, start your own retirement group.

There are two exciting benefits to starting a group. One, you cut quickly to the real underlying issues involved in the retirement transition process, which provides personal relief and release. And the second is the incredible friendships you can make with other Transitioners.

Men's Night Out

Derek Moore

Derek Moore created his own group.

"At the insistence of our wives, two friends and I started to host a Men's Night Out so that we and our longtime friends could add some mid-week interest to our lives with an evening of poker, pool, darts and beer.

"The first three Men's Nights were well received and the guy talk consisted of the usual mixture of sports, politics and investments. The evenings generally broke up around 1:00 a.m. with everyone having had a good time. On the fourth one, though, something unusual happened when the conversation turned to retirement.

"The unretired guys were shocked and in disbelief when they discovered that their retired friends were not as happy as they had supposed. The retired guys were surprised and relieved to discover that they were not alone in experiencing relationship, space and accountability issues with their wives after retirement. The conversation was electric and went on until 3:30 a.m.

"When the guys left, they knew they had broken new ground. They had admitted to personal problems. They were discovering each other for the first time, in many cases after 25 years of friendship. And they were discovering what their wives knew all along: they could be a support group for each other.

"We have now held over a dozen Men's Nights and we typically draw a crowd of 15 or so guys, mostly retired. To some it is just a good night out, but to others of us it is an opportunity to unwind and share problems in a safe environment. We are strengthening our friendships, seeing each other in a truer light, learning from each other and even supporting each other. Will the next step be caring for each other? Who knows, but the guys are all ready for their next Men's Night Out.

How to Start Your Own Group
Gather a group of acquaintances as Derek did, or consider starting a group at your church, synagogue or community center. We have taught classes in all of those locations, both in and out of the city. They have always been well attended.

"Life deserves to be celebrated. It's our way of saying thank you."
Barbara Lazear Ascher, Delphinium Books

- *Announce your group.* Publicize the formation of your group in the organization's bulletin. People can choose to join. Those who self-select make very interested participants.

- *Facilitate.* Don't try to teach. Ask questions and stay quiet to allow as many voices as possible to be heard. The sharing is what builds confidence and leads to solutions for this transition. Small groups of about 12 to 14 work best. This allows enough time in a one-hour meeting for each attendee to speak about his or her varied experiences.

- *Use this book as a workbook.* Review a chapter each session. Write the questions at the beginning of each session on the board and use them to lead the discussion. Conclude with the Discovery Exercises. Pass them out at one session. Discuss the answers at the next.

- *Start the first class with introductions.* After you introduce yourself talk about how you made the decision to facilitate a class and tell them something about you and your retirement. Introduce the class by reviewing the topics you will discuss each week. Ask participants to introduce themselves, tell their most recent place of employment, and share their reasons for attending the class. If there is any time left, start the session with a question like "What is your toughest issue?" or "What was your biggest surprise?"

- *Get a timekeeper.* A must-have for your group, however, is a timekeeper. Once the conversation gets going, it can take off. Be friendly, but tough. If one person tries to dominate the conversation, others will stop coming.

- *Determine the length.* Our classes at Emory University's Academy for Retired Professionals have been eight-week sessions. But, fewer sessions can work as well. Often the most interested continue to meet long after the sessions have ended. (One class met monthly for the entire year!)

- *Let us know how you're doing.* www.CelebrateRetirement.com

Discovery Exercise 24

How Are You Giving Back?

Instructions: List the many ways you are giving back by helping others. List the places and causes you choose to serve going forward.

What skills and talents do you have to offer to an agency or an individual?
What can you do to help someone or some organization reach their goals?

_____

_____

_____

_____

_____

On what projects or committees do you serve?

_____

_____

_____

_____

How can you serve as a donor? *Blood, canned goods, expertise, equipment, etc.*

_____

_____

_____

_____

What fund-raising efforts do you support?

_____

_____

_____

_____

_____

On what non-profit boards do you serve?

_____

_____

_____

_____

What impact have you had? Where do you see a need for change?

_____

_____

_____

_____

_____

_____

_____

_____

Solutions from Survivors
on Making a Difference

Q. I climbed the corporate ladder for 25 years to the exclusion of almost everything else. Now that I'm retired I'm having a difficult time volunteering. My style is too aggressive for the organizations I've volunteered with and the organizations are too loosely and inefficiently managed for me to get much satisfaction. Help!

A. Many agencies have professional staffs and regard transitioning executives as challengers or intruders. Agencies succeed on consensus, not profits. It may take longer to accomplish goals than a hard-charging executive is accustomed to. Staff members may feel threatened by volunteer ideas and initiatives.

If there isn't a fit for your skills, keep looking. Your contributions, experience and talents demand that you find the right outlet. It may take a while.

Q. I'd like to commit some of my time and resources to an organization I care about, but my wife doesn't want me to. Any suggestions?

A. Spend some real time discovering her objections. Does she think the agency is legitimate? Does she want the funds to go to something she is interested in? Is she nervous about retirement money running out? Is she unwilling to share? Value her reasoning, but if you still feel strongly, honor your gut feelings. It's your retirement. Take control.

Q. I have many years of business experience and would like to help others start a business or grow in their career. I'd like some help getting started.

A. One of our engineer classmates had always wanted to teach and volunteered to give a class at a learning center. Another Reinventing Retirement student offered to help him, and they developed retirement lifestyle classes for pre-retirees with a financial planner.

Or, work as a volunteer for SCORE, Counselors to America's Small Business. SCORE volunteers are active and retired individuals who have business experience. They share their knowledge with current and potential entrepreneurs. Being a SCORE counselor is the perfect opportunity for active or retired business owners to use their skills while helping the local economy prosper.

You can learn more about volunteer opportunities at *www.score.org*.

Q. I received a large sum of money when I retired and want to set up a Charitable Trust Fund, but I don't want the hassle of record keeping or the IRS.

A. Community Trust Funds are a simple and affordable way to give without the pain of paperwork.

Community Foundations are made up of a pool of donors. Because they administer funds from many donors rather than just one, they are usually classified under the tax code as public charities and therefore are subject to different rules and regulations than those that govern private foundations.

They will administer your funds wherever you choose and handle the paperwork for a small percentage of the assets. Because Community Foundations work to identify and prioritize the needs of your community, they can identify the most critical community needs for you.

Community Foundations may also be a place to discover volunteer opportunities for you or your family. Check the Yellow Pages or Internet for foundations in your area.

Loose Ends

Notes

_____

_____

_____

Questions

_____

_____

_____

Ideas

_____

_____

_____

Favorite Resources

_____

_____

_____

Things to Share on the Web Page CelebrateRetirement.com

_____

_____

_____

CHAPTER 8

Becoming a Work in Progress

Retirement today creates new cause for celebration. As Transitioners discover that they may spend more time in this stage than any previous retirees, they have a unique opportunity to get it right the second time. This gives people fresh drive and determination to explore new locations, investigate new interests and to renew a lifetime of meaningful relationships.

Retirement means freedom for all and frustrations for some. Every life celebration — from birthdays, college graduations, marriages and career promotions, to the birth (or death) of a loved one — comes with change. And, with that change comes the loss of the familiar and fear of the new. It's called growth. It's normal, but it's disquieting.

Those who attended the Reinventing Retirement workshops were celebrating their freedom, dealing with their frustrations, yet itching for something more.

They came armed with notebooks and pens expecting to be given a clear plan for figuring out this remarkable stage of life. What they discovered is that their plan comes from within. Only they could address their long-neglected needs; their desire to use their skills and talents in a new way.

What's This Transition Thing *Really* Like?

Marla Church

Marla Church, transitioning patent attorney, sums up the transition best.

"Reflecting back on my retirement three years ago, I can see that the adjustment just took time. The first six months were euphoric. Trips to the Winter Olympics, Japan and a new kitchen were exciting and kept me busy. Then the trips were over. I was carrying extra pounds (the new kitchen appliances really did work) and my husband was at work. That's when the transition reality hit. Now what? I literally ran to a part-time job to fill my time and give purpose to my days.

"I *really* needed to talk with others who were also dealing with retirement experiences. Enter the Reinventing Retirement class: a roomful of Transitioners who wanted to talk and share their experiences.

"Now three years later, I am bringing it all together. The part-time job has served its purpose and I've moved on. A rigorous physical fitness program provides new challenges, a schedule, and an external family of fitness buffs for support. The side effects are a lot better than what one gets from sitting at a desk all day.

"I use my recently acquired Japanese every week at our favorite sushi bar and we are spending Thanksgiving in Egypt this year. I think Archeology 101 will be my next challenge!"

Bringing It Together

The Entrepreneur and the Corporate Exec

No two people celebrate retirement in the same way. There is no "one size fits all" approach to a life without business pressures. Transitioners in the class start new businesses; take off on skiing, hiking or biking adventures; reclaim forgotten passions or find new ones.

Exploring these options is absorbing. When most of us left college or graduate school we tightly focused on a "get a job" future. We exited work as independent individuals with a lot less peer pressure. Each happily chooses a different door to walk through.

The Entrepreneur

Wicke Chambers

My celebration into retirement began with the need for a rebirth, a renaissance of spirit. I wanted to enjoy my third stage of life and sow the seeds of my own legacy. I wanted to contribute, get involved in a new way, become an adventurer, feel celebratory. Mission Accomplished!

But...it...just...took...time. Almost five years.

Being "open to possibilities" worked for me. I couldn't have written a plan that would have led me to today. I could never have imagined getting a new partner and getting so involved in the subject of retirement that it produced a series of classes and a seventh book.

I could never have envision leading workshops on the subject to learn from generous and spirited other Transitioners who were also celebratory and frustrated like me – many of whom now have become new buddies. I never envisioned the research trips to talk to experts in the field or going off to national seminars, being written up in a *Wall Street Journal Encore* publication or participating in an NBC *Nightly News* broadcast.

I didn't have a clue how about how to evolve. It just became my lifestyle.

Reinventing myself is now my new Golden Rule. I will never "retire" in the classic sense. Retirement may be my category, but not my attitude.

There are so many fascinating and exciting things to explore. For now, I'm a world traveler with my husband, an energetic golfer and grandmother, a board member, a Free Cell player, and an "ageless explorer."

I relish having the time to enjoy twenty minutes in a parking lot catching up with an elementary school friend or spending time with seven grandchildren with seven distinct interests.

But what adds richness to this period is learning to spend my newfound time in little, meaningful ways. Before I go to sleep each night I tick off five things I'm most grateful for about my day. Now there are a lot more than five.

The Corporate Exec

Cheryl Stephenson

"When I retired at age 52, I couldn't believe my good fortune. I felt like I'd caught the golden ring and couldn't wait to see what life had in store.

I threw myself into the freedom and fun. A celebratory trip to the Idaho wilderness with a group of friends; two trips to Europe; regular visits to Florida to spend time with the new man in my life. I enjoyed a whirlwind year before coasting to a stop.

I realized to my surprise that I needed more. Challenging projects. Interesting people. Mental stimulation.

A chance meeting at Rotary led me to a non-profit agency that taught kids about international business. I enjoyed helping develop a strategic business plan, a new web site and a fundraising plan.

Through that experience I met a publisher and author, and had the opportunity to try my hand at marketing two sports magazines. Other part-time and volunteer adventures followed. I edited a legal guide for women in Georgia; helped develop a sports hall of fame; and have written successful grants for an organization that cares for abused and neglected children.

Through it all, I've tried to make heads or tails of this life transition called retirement, and to help others enjoy the freedom and minimize the frustrations it often brings. The day three participants in a pre-retirement seminar gave me after-class hugs, I realized that helping others is a far greater thrill than any business accomplishment.

Most importantly, retirement's given me a second chance to know and love my family. Baking with my mother is always a sticky mess, but the rewards are sweet.

Hauling shrubs, mulch or other landscaping material in my Dad's old truck gives us time to talk or just enjoy the ride. Even doctor visits and time spent in waiting rooms (and there have been a few) have reinforced the importance of family and having someone to lean on when times get tough.

I've reconnected with old friends, met new ones and now have time for both. I'm learning to play. Explore. Satisfy my curiosity about the world around me. And, I'm counting the months until my Florida beau retires.

For me, retirement has been a journey to find myself. There have been surprises around every bend, over every hill. And, I love the possibilities of an open road.

Two New "Works in Progress"

We have been in our transition process for five years. What started as our own need to learn from other survivors how to make this stage of life fresh has become a full-blown pursuit and passion.

Writing *Celebrate Retirement, The Freedom and the Frustrations* has been a celebration, a labor of love, and an opportunity to share exciting discoveries about this rarely discussed, almost taboo subject with newly acquired friends.

The next adventure is www.CelebrateRetirement.com, a web site that connects the celebratory and the frustrated on the site. Transitioners can post insights, questions and "ah-has" to continue to learn from each other how to celebrate this new stage of life and how to deal with the frustrations. Together we will help each other to make meaningful choices, and to use our well-honed business skills to discover new peers, exciting interests, and purposeful work. Most of all, to encourage each of us to take the time to discover what makes us come alive.

This book is designed to give you new ways to celebrate your freedom, ease your frustrations, empower you to be bold in making meaningful choices, and to energize you to use your corporate skills to discover new peers, exciting interests, and purposeful work.

Discovery Exercise 25

Your Celebration Plan

Instructions: Having a plan will help you move toward the retirement of your dreams. In the spaces below, write down what you'd like to do, then make it happen!

In the next month I'd like to:

_____

_____

_____

What action steps does that involve?

_____

_____

_____

Any obstacles?

_____

_____

_____

In the next six months I'd like to:

_____

_____

_____

What action steps does that involve?

_____

_____

_____

Any obstacles?

_____

_____

_____

In the next year I'd like to:

_____

_____

_____

What action steps does that involve?

_____

_____

_____

Any obstacles?

_____

_____

_____

Eleven Kick-Ass Solutions from Survivors

1. Get a Transition Buddy to help you handle the peaks and pits of the transition.

2. Remember that this transition thing is just a process. It's not a life sentence. Like grief, the terrible twos or a hangover, it will pass. It just takes time.

3. Explore the essential needs that work satisfied. Replace your work family with your own family, replace business challenges with labors of love.

4. Shed your business identity. Don't be afraid to climb out of your business box and move from guru status to novice, learner, or apprentice in a new field.

5. Deal with time management by filling your life with golf balls, not sand.

6. Stamp out the "busy-ness junkie" within that comes from racing to meet other people's demands. Think daily about what you do for yourself.

7. Get a grip on your relationships. They can be a blessing or a curse. Spend time with those who make you laugh and feel good *before you visit those who don't.*

8. Realize that life doesn't stop when you stop working.

9. Embrace your opportunity to give back. It's the stuff legacies are made of.

10. Celebrate your new status: *A Work In Progress.* Set up orange cones around your work space, strap on your tool belt, and enjoy whatever pursuits give you joy and make you come alive.

11. Above all else, remember "If it's to be, it's up to me."

About the Authors

Wicke Chambers is the co-founder with Spring Asher of Chambers & Asher Speechworks, an internationally known firm specializing in speech and media training. They wrote "Getting Ahead," a business column in the *Atlanta Journal/Constitution* for four years. In television, she and Asher won six Emmy Awards and the Best of Gannett Award for news programming. She has one great husband, three cherished children and seven lively grandchildren who live happily in Atlanta.

Cheryl Stephenson is a public relations executive with 30 years in the public, private and non-profit sectors. She developed a nationally recognized community relations program for Southwire Company, and her work has been honored 22 times by the Public Relations Society of America, the International Association of Business Communicators and Women in Communications. She volunteers, consults and sleeps late in Newnan, Georgia.

Winslow Press
Order Form

E-mail orders: orders@CelebrateRetirement.com

Telephone orders: Call 770-254-8352. Please have Visa or MasterCard number, expiration date, name, mailing address, and daytime telephone number ready. *Books are mailed within three working days.*

Mail orders: Make checks payable to Winslow Press, LLC. Send order form with check to Winslow Press, 140 South Shore Drive, Newnan, Georgia 30263.

Please send _____ copies of *Celebrate Retirement, The Freedom and the Frustrations.*

If not satisfied, I understand that I may return the book for a full refund.

Name: _____

Address: _____

City: _____ State: _____ ZIP: _____

Telephone: _____

e-mail address: _____

Sales Tax: Please add 7% sales tax for products shipped to Georgia addresses.

Shipping:
U.S.: $4.00 for first book and $2.00 for each additional book.
International: $9.00 for first book and $5.00 for each additional book.